# BUILDERS OF NEW ZEALAND

Logging with Bullock Team and Horse Tramway  *Alexander Turnbull Library*

# BUILDERS OF NEW ZEALAND

## by A.W. Reed

*An Illustrated History for Young People*

A.H. & A.W. REED

*First published 1972*

A. H. & A. W. REED LTD.

182 Wakefield Street, Wellington
51 Whiting Street, Artarmon, Sydney
111 Southampton Row, London, WC1
also
29 Dacre Street, Auckland
165 Cashel Street, Christchurch

© 1972 LITERARY PRODUCTIONS LTD

ISBN: 0 589 04716 7

Set by New Zealand Typesetters Ltd, Wellington
Printed offset by Dai Nippon Printing Co. (International) Ltd., Hong Kong

# Acknowledgments

The publishers are indebted to several artists whose work has previously appeared in series of educational and general publications.

Beatrice Foster-Barham: endpapers

T. T. Barrow: pages 14, 15

Russell Clark: pages 29, 30, 31, 32, 33, 39, 40, 41, 42, 43, 45, 46, 47, 48, 49, 51, 52, 53, 55, 56, 58, 62, 63, 64, 65, 66, 67, 68, 69, 70, 71, 72, 73, 74, 75, 76, 77, 79, 80, 81

A. G. Collins, redrawn by R. Labone: pages 93, 136, 151

H. D. B. Dansey: pages 11, 13, 16, 17, 18, 23, 24, 25, 26, 46

W. Dittmer: pages 12, 20

L. C. Mitchell: pages 139, 144

Dennis Turner: pages 27, 44

Thanks are also due to the following:

*K. and J. Bigwood* for permission to reproduce the photograph on page 149.

*Dominion Museum, Wellington*, for permission to reproduce the illustrations that appear on pages 33 to 39 and on page 45. They were drawn by artists employed by the Museum, and appeared previously in *Maori Life and Custom* by W. J. Phillipps.

*Alexander Turnbull Library, Wellington*, for permission to include the photographs, engravings, and drawings on pages 49, 54, 61, 83, 86 to 140, 142, 143, 145, 147.

*Ministry of Works* for permission to include the architectural drawing on page 121.

*National Publicity Studios, Wellington*, for permission to include the photographs on pages 52, 56, 123, 141, 143, 148, 153, 155, and for the cover picture by Marcus King of the Signing of the Treaty of Waitangi.

*NZ Government Railways* for permission to include photographs on pages 143 and 146. The maps on pages 10 and 157 were drawn by Julius Petro.

*Otago Early Settlers' Association* for permission to reproduce the painting on page 125.

*The Hocken Library, Dunedin*, for permission to include illustrations on pages 102 and 113.

*To my Californian grandson*
*SCOTT ALEXANDER REED*

# Contents

## Chapter One  HOW THE MAORIS CAME TO NEW ZEALAND

### The Homeland

When white men from Europe first sailed into the Pacific Ocean they found that many of the islands were inhabited by graceful, dark-haired, brown-skinned folk who were later called Polynesians. "Polynesia" comes from two Greek words meaning "many islands". If you look at the map you will see a triangle that encloses all the islands from Hawaii in the north to New Zealand in the south-west and Easter Island in the east.

It was on the thousands of islands inside this triangle that these people lived. The European explorers found that although the islands were separated by thousands of kilometres of sea, all the Polynesian people spoke similar languages, had many of the same customs, worshipped the same gods, and used similar tools. When Captain Cook came to New Zealand and met the Maori people for the first time, he brought with him from the island of Tahiti,

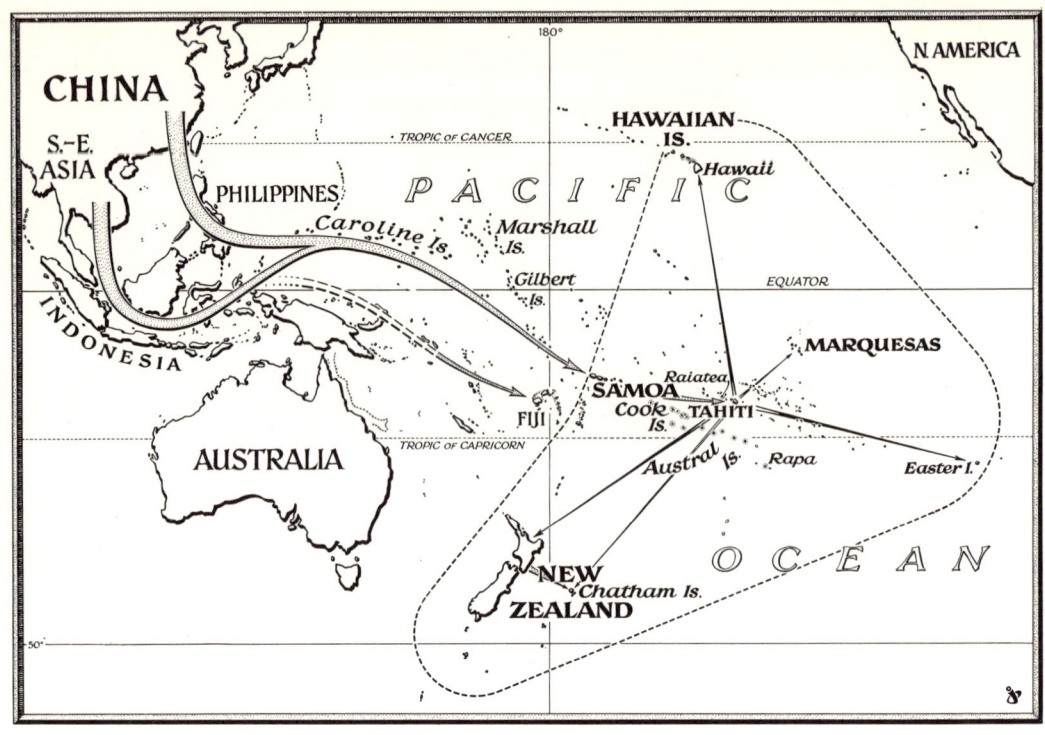

more than 4,000 kilometres away, the priest Tupaea who could understand the language of the Maoris.

For almost 200 years men have been asking, "Where did the
Maori and Polynesian people come from, and how did they reach
their island homes?" Thousands of years ago, we are now told,
crowds of people began to migrate into south-east Asia from the
north and north-west. As they moved in the local inhabitants were
driven out of Asia in several places. As the pressure built up behind
them, these earlier people were forced to sail further and further away
from the shores of their Asian homeland and into the thousands
of islands of the Pacific Ocean. In this way we believe that the
wanderings of the Polynesians must have begun. Many hundreds
of years later the first European navigators found these people in
the "many islands" of Polynesia. During the centuries of their
passage through Indonesia they became hardy seamen and learned
how to build large sea-going canoes.

The first Polynesians probably came down through the "tiny
islands" of Micronesia and settled, first in Samoa and Tonga, and

10

then in Tahiti. From an island in the Tahiti group called in ancient times Hawaiki, and now known as Ra'iatea, came groups of hardy sailors with their wives, families, and livestock to settle the islands of New Zealand. They called the country Aotearoa, and there they became the Maori people who today live and work beside their Pakeha friends.

Before we read about these vast journeyings, where ancient legends and stories alone can provide history books, let us try to picture the great seaworthy canoes of the Vikings of the Sunrise. Some were double canoes, and others had one or two outriggers. Some were over 30 metres in length and were manned by a crew of as many as 140 men.

Many of the double canoes had a small house built on a platform connecting the two canoes. There was little space to sleep, but regular watches were kept, so that there was no need to find room for the whole crew to sleep at one time. The hollow tree trunks that formed the canoes had their sides built up with slabs of wood joined neatly together, each plank being sewn to the next with woven or plaited cord which was passed through holes in the planks. Thwarts, which were also used as seats for the paddlers, were lashed to the planks and helped to strengthen the vessel. In bad weather the canoes rode out the storm by means of sea anchors, with others at the stern to keep the bow head on to the waves. The paddles were long and pointed. With sails set, the canoes could cover long distances in a short time.

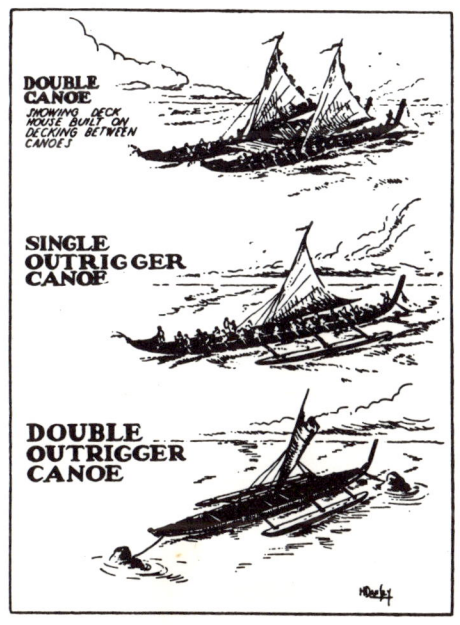

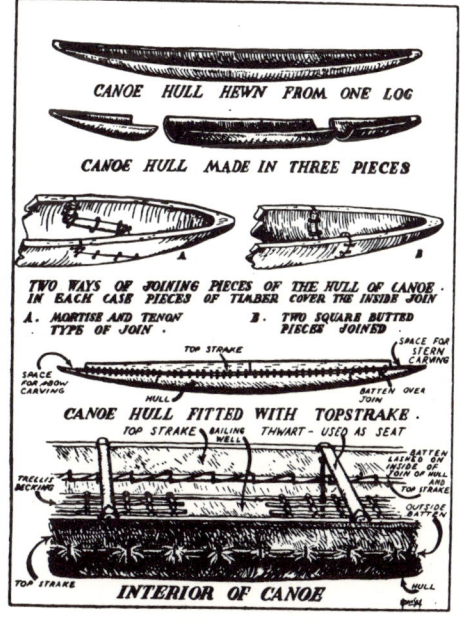

## The First Voyage

If we go far back in time, even before William the Conqueror invaded England, we can find traditions that tell us that Maui, half god and half sea rover, sailed into the southern seas and pulled New Zealand, like a great fish, out of the water.

Some people believe this is a poetic way of saying that he discovered the country; but the Maoris said that the South Island was Maui's canoe and Stewart Island its anchor, while as for the North Island, anyone can see that it is a fish, for its tail points northwards, it has Taupo Moana for its heart, and Wellington Harbour and Lake Wairarapa for its eyes. Even the fishhook is there in the curving bight of Hawke Bay. Te Ika-nui-a-Maui is its name – The Great Fish of Maui.

# The Legend of Kupe and Ngahue

It was the wife of Kupe who first named the new land when it rose from the sea after her husband's canoe had spent many days and nights of voyaging a thousand years ago. "He ao! He ao!", "A cloud! A cloud!" she cried, and as they sailed on the cloud grew into a long bright world, into a land of long-lingering daylight – Aotearoa! We must never forget those first pioneers and their canoes, Kupe in the Matahorua and his companion Ngahue in the Tawiri-rangi. They are the first explorers and the first canoes of our island history.

Matahorua and Tawiri-rangi made their landfall in the far north and sailed down the east coast, landing at places that we now know as Castlepoint and Palliser Bay, and sailed into Wellington Harbour. Their camp fires twinkled under the karaka trees in the bush at Seatoun where the headlights of cars now sweep along the waterfront.

Leaving Wellington, the canoes sailed through the strait to Porirua. After a brief visit to the South Island, full of exciting adventures, they turned their prows towards their island homeland. They sailed up the west coast and left the shores of Aotearoa from Hokianga, "Kupe's Returning Place", crossed the ocean to Rarotonga, and at last arrived back in Hawaiki.

"It is a wonderful land that we have discovered," Kupe said. "The forests cover the islands from the sea to the great mountain ranges that shine as white as sea-foam in the sun. The song of birds is heard everywhere. There are no fierce beasts, only the moa."

His listeners laughed, for they knew the moa only as a tame, plump fowl.

"You would not laugh if you saw it," Kupe said. "It is a great, fierce bird, twice the height of a man. Look, I will show you!" He ran to his canoe and, unwrapping a bundle, showed them a piece of preserved flesh and told them how Ngahue had driven the bird into a corner and killed it. "Now show them the pounamu," he commanded Ngahue. His friend unwrapped a smaller parcel and held out the dark, gleaming jade that he had found at Arahura. "It is hard and bright and shining," he said. "It will make weapons for warfare, and ornaments to wear."

And so it did, for from the piece of greenstone that Ngahue had brought were made a hei-tiki, an ear-pendant, and two adzes which, centuries later, were used to make some of the canoes of the Great Migration.

A Tahitian voyaging canoe with double hull and furled sails

# The Moa-Hunters

While they were exploring New Zealand, Kupe and Ngahue saw no people, but we must remember that they were here only for a short time and that they could not have seen much of the country. There were people living here at that time. We do not know very much about them, though new discoveries are telling us something of how they lived. Because they hunted the moa for food, we call them the "moa-hunters". They were Polynesians, but we cannot be quite sure where they came from.

What we do know is that they lived in New Zealand more than a thousand years ago; that they lived mostly at the mouth of rivers in both the North and South Islands; that they used ornaments made from moa bones; that they put the eggs of moas in the graves of dead chiefs; that they drew pictures on the walls of caves; and that they were a peace-loving people. Scientists called archaeologists have found places where the moa-hunters threw the bones after eating food. These bone deposits are called middens, and they tell us a great deal about the food that the moa-hunters ate. We know that they ate moas, of course, and other large birds that once lived in New Zealand but that are now extinct. They also ate seals and dogs. Dogs were not native animals, so they must have brought these animals with them when they came to New Zealand.

When the Fleet Maoris (whom you will read about later) arrived, they were surprised to find that there were people living here. They called them tangata whenua, or people of the land, and were inclined to look down on them, but they intermarried with them, and in time formed one people whom we now know as Maoris. This feeling of superiority led the later Maoris to claim descent from their famous ancestors who had come in the Fleet, and to forget about the ancestors who were of the tangata whenua.

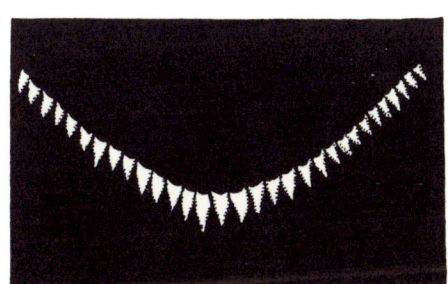

Necklace of shark's teeth

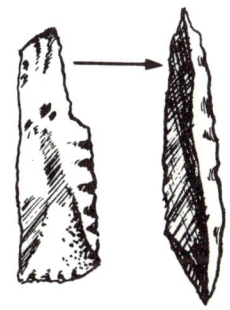

A stone adze

Moa-hunter artifacts

# Toi and Whatonga

The years passed by as generation after generation made themselves at home in Kupe's fabled land. About thirty generations ago a canoe race was held in the lagoon Pikopiko-i-whiti in Hawaiki. The old chief Toi sat on the slopes of a hill to watch the race. His grandson Whatonga and his young friend Tu Rahui were in command of one of the canoes.

Whatonga and Tu Rahui and their men won the race. They swept through the gap in the reef and into the open sea; but before they could return a sudden storm rose and they were forced to run before it. Day after day Toi kept watch for the return of his grandson, but in vain. When he had given up hope of their return he prepared his own canoe, Te Paepae-ki-Rarotonga, and went in search of the lost canoe. Te Paepae-ki-Rarotonga was the pride of the tribe, and there were a hundred men eager to serve under Toi. They sailed westwards and in a few days reached a strange island. Whatonga had been there, and Toi found some of the crew living on the island.

"Where is my grandson?" he asked eagerly, but they could not tell him.

"He has sailed on these many days, but we do not know where he went."

"Perhaps he has gone to Kupe's land," Toi said.

The old warrior set out for the southern islands. He called at Rarotonga on the way and then sailed southwards. When land was sighted the old man's hopes rose, but he soon found that these were the smaller, less hospitable islands known today as the Chathams. After a short stay the sails were hoisted again, and Toi arrived at Aotearoa, landing at Tamaki which is part of the present city of Auckland.

Toi made inquiries amongst the tangata whenua, but he could learn nothing about Whatonga and Tu Rahui, so he made his home at Whakatane, far from the people he knew and loved, his

only neighbours being the despised tangata whenua. Instead of the tasty kumaras and the luscious tropical fruits he was used to eating, he and his people had to depend on the products of the forest, on fern-root, and dishes of fowl and fish. The tangata whenua gave him a name by which he is affectionately remembered – Toi-kai-rakau, or Toi the Wood-eater.

In the meantime Whatonga had made his way back to Hawaiki, only to find that his grandfather had left in search of him.

"Can my love be less for Toi than that of Toi for me?" he asked. His canoe, Te Hawai, was renamed Kurahaupo and made ready for sea. With a crew of sixty men and several women Whatonga set out on his quest.

In island after island he heard news of Toi until at length he was sure that the old man had gone to Aotearoa. The Kurahaupo landed on the west coast at Tongaporutu, and there he heard stories that had spread far and wide of Toi-kai-rakau who lived at Whakatane. In great excitement the crew sailed northwards, rounded the northern end of the island, and at length landed at Maketu in the Bay of Plenty. Whatonga found Toi living in a pa maioro (a fortified village with earthwork defences), called Kapu-te-rangi, on a hill overlooking the present township of Whakatane.

Whatonga eventually moved to Mahia and in his old age his sons Tara and Tautoki settled at Wellington Harbour which was named Te Whanganui-a-Tara, the Great Harbour of Tara. The descendants of the people of Toi and Whatonga were known as Te Tini-o-Toi, the Multitudes of Toi; and so the settlement of New Zealand by the Maori people began.

# *Manaia*

While Whatonga was searching for his grandfather, two chiefs in Hawaiki named Nuku and Manaia were at war. As he was the weaker of the two, Manaia made his escape in the Tokomaru canoe. Nuku and his people pursued the conquered chief in the canoes Te Houama, Waimate, and Tangi-apakura.

Manaia and Nuku both called at Rarotonga and then came on to Aotearoa. Manaia passed through the strait that separates the two islands and landed at Rangitoto (D'Urville Island). When Nuku arrived Manaia had gone but the ashes of the camp fire were still warm. The chase continued until Manaia was sighted at Pukerua, a sheltered bay on the rocky coast a few miles north of Wellington. Nuku caught up with Manaia and there was a terrible fight that lasted until darkness fell.

The two chiefs, calling to one another across the water, agreed to land and spend the night at rest, resuming the battle the next day. They went ashore at Paekakariki, but all that night a fierce gale raged and the breakers thundered on the shore. The storm was caused by Manaia who had called on the god of the sea to help him. When morning came it was found that the rollers had piled up the sand into dunes which stretched from Paekakariki to Otaki, and were known as Te Ahuahu-a-Manaia. Nuku's canoes were smashed and his fighting strength broken, so peace was declared. Nuku returned to Hawaiki when he had repaired the canoes, but Manaia remained in Aotearoa and formed the third settlement of Polynesian people. He stayed at the bay called Tokomaru; which was named after his canoe. Later he went to Tongaporutu, a little while after Whatonga's visit.

For the next 200 years legends tell us of crossings and recrossings of the southern seas. Little is known of these voyages or of the men who made them. During that time it is possible that supplies of kumaras were imported, and that the tubers provided seed for the extensive kumara plantations of the North Island.

# Accidental Voyages

On sunny days, with light favourable breezes, voyages were often made by canoe from one Pacific island to another for barter or to visit friends and relatives. Large canoes sometimes went out on raiding expeditions, especially when food was scarce; and in most weathers fishing canoes put out to sea so that the villagers might have plenty of fish to eat. The fishermen looked at the stars and observed the winds and currents when they were at sea, but usually they tried to keep in sight of land. This was not difficult, especially where volcanic peaks lifted high above the horizon. In this way men and women travelled from one island to another and found new homes when their own small islands became crowded and there was not enough food for their needs.

Some people think that the boldest sailors made long voyages of discovery far from land, and that the islands of New Zealand, so far distant from the homeland, were discovered in this way. This is what the Maoris themselves believed. There are many legends that tell of tremendous journeys from Hawaiki to Aotearoa, and even of return voyages.

In recent years other people have come to believe that the Polynesians were not able to make long, planned voyages, even though they possessed large ocean-going canoes. They had no compass, and on a long voyage no one could depend on the direction of wind and wave. No, say these people, the long voyages of colonisation were made accidentally. Sudden storms would blow up, and the canoes might drift many hundreds of kilometres until they were lost in the cruel sea. But every now and then a storm-tossed canoe might drift ashore somewhere. In this way new islands were discovered, but there was little chance of the shipwrecked sailors ever finding their way home again. The voyages to New Zealand, these people say, were "drift voyages". Some of the canoes must have had women on board as well as men, and so children were born and the Maori people of New Zealand, few in number at first, gradually populated these far-away islands.

No one can be quite sure that the early arrivals came to these shores accidentally, nor can anyone be sure that they planned their journeys in advance. The Maoris themselves had no doubts. The stories that follow are the legendary accounts that tell how the Maoris came to New Zealand during what is known as the Heke, or Great Migration.

THE COMING OF THE MAORI

## *The Arawa Canoe*

It is from the Great Migration, or the coming of the Fleet, about 600 years ago, that the Maori loves to trace his descent. Fierce wars had broken out in the tropic islands. Over-population and shortage of food were the principal causes. For these and other reasons a brave company of people set sail in their picturesquely-named canoes – Te Arawa (The Shark), Tainui (Great Tide), Mataatua (Face of a God), Kurahaupo (Storm Cloud), and Tokomaru (Staff

20

of the War-god). In addition there were the Aotea, Takitimu, and Horouta, which sailed about the same time, but did not accompany the main fleet.

The canoes moved restlessly as the triangular sails were hoisted, and cries of grief and farewell rose above the soughing of the trade wind in the palms. A sudden hush had fallen. Where the wavelets lapped the sand stood the grey-haired patriarch Hou-mai-tawhiti. He lifted his voice in the poroporoaki, the farewell speech: "Follow not after the god of war in your country of the south; hold to the deeds of Rongo the Peaceful. Haere! Haere! Haere atu ra!"

His voice faded into silence. The wind bore it away until it was lost. The little waves caressed the canoes as they slid away from the shore. Te Arawa led the way, her three sails carrying her swiftly out to sea. The other canoes followed, fading into the distance one by one, frail-winged birds that dared the perils of the ocean.

The Arawa was the leading canoe. Tama-te-kapua, Son of the Clouds, was her captain. He was unlike his gentle father, for he carried the war-god in his heart. He chuckled to himself as the Arawa lifted to the long ocean swell. Before leaving he had asked Ngatoro-i-rangi, the famous tohunga, to come aboard to perform the sacred rites that would ensure the protection of the atua (gods) for his canoe. Ngatoro had come unsuspectingly, bringing his wife Kearoa with him. As soon as they set foot in the canoe Tama-te-kapua had ordered the sails to be raised, and while the priest and his wife were protesting, they were sailing beyond the reach of the other canoes. This was the reason why Te Arawa had led the way out of the harbour.

One day Ngatoro climbed on to the roof of the house built between the two canoes of the double vessel and called aloud to the gods. His magic power went out from the lonely vessel, and strong winds blew out of a clear sky. The canoe turned its prow towards Te Korokoro-o-te-Parata, the Throat of the Sea-monster. Waves licked fiercely at the Arawa, the sky became dull and heavy, and the canoe was drawn into the outer spiral of a maelstrom. The carved prow disappeared, the water reached the first bailing place, and then the second in the middle of the canoe. From the roof of the house Ngatoro heard the wooden gods splashing into the water and saw the crew grasping the thwarts to save themselves from being thrown out. At length he took pity on them and asked Tangaroa, the sea-god, for his protection. Gradually the wide throat of Te Parata closed and the surging waters grew calm once more.

After many days they came in sight of land. As the canoe glided into a peaceful harbour, the water was like glass, reflecting the blazing glory of the flowering pohutukawa trees. The crimson blossoms rivalled the bright colour of the head ornaments of the crew. One of the men threw his kura, a prized ornament of red feathers, into the sea and cried, "See there, red ornaments for the head are more plentiful in this country than in Hawaiki." He was bitterly disappointed when he found that the glowing colour came from flowers that withered almost as soon as they were placed in the hair, and crumbled at a touch.

Tainui and Te Arawa arrived about the same time. Forgetting the parting words of Hou-mai-tawhiti, the commanders quarrelled over the claim to be the first arrival. A whale was stranded on the beach and the captain of each canoe claimed it as his property. It was because of this whale that the bay, tucked under the sheltering point of Cape Runaway, was named Whangaparaoa, the Bay of the Sperm Whale. An inspection was made of the sacred places that had been set up on the shore by the crew, and it was found that while the posts set up by the men of Tainui were weathered and dried, those of Te Arawa were fresh and green. Tainui therefore claimed the honour of being the first arrivals and the ownership of the whale. All that it proved, however, was that the men of Tainui were the more cunning, for they had secretly passed the posts and ropes through a fire, which gave them a weathered appearance. Tainui had in fact arrived after Te Arawa. The crew had also put their mooring rope under that of the Arawa canoe; and for these reasons it was admitted that Tainui must have been the first canoe to arrive!

The Arawa people had brought kumaras with them, and some were planted at Whangaparaoa where they grow to this day. Shortly afterwards the canoe continued its voyage. Under the command of the chief Taikehu, 140 men explored the north-west coast. The Arawa then sailed to the island of Motiti. At Maketu the people set up their altar. There are rocks at Maketu that are said to be the bow and stern pieces of the Arawa. The stern anchor, Tu-te-rangi-karuru, is a solid outcrop to which the anchor was probably fastened. The descendants of Tama-te-kapua peopled the Hot Lakes district, while Ngatoro and his followers went to Lake Taupo; and so it is said of the Arawa canoe that the prow is Maketu and the stern-post Tongariro.

Tama-te-kapua was restless at Maketu. He went north and joined forces with Taikehu at Tauranga. After a while he went on to Hauraki and Colville, and at the cape at the tip of the Coromandel Peninsula he made his home, and there he died. Ngatoro and his wife had settled on Motiti Island, while Tama was buried by his sons on the forested ridge of Moehau.

When they buried him his sons said, "Let him slumber here where his spirit can gaze far over the ocean and over the land of Aotearoa. The winds that sweep across the great ocean of Kiwa, they shall ever sing his oriori, his lullaby."

It was a fitting funeral song for the famous sailor. His memorial is in the name that the Maoris have preserved for the cape – Te Moe-hau-o-Tama-te-kapua, Tama's Windy Sleeping Place.

Tama-te-kapua had two brothers named Tia and Hei. Tia was the discoverer of Taupo (Taupo-nui-a-Tia), and Hei settled at Whitianga.

The burning of the Arawa canoe

# The Tainui, Mataatua, and Kurahaupo Canoes

The Tainui canoe was built after the Arawa. There was bitterness of feeling between the men of the two canoes after Tama's treachery in abducting Ngatoro and his wife. The Tainui, like the Arawa, was a double canoe, and Hoturoa was her captain. After leaving Whanga-paraoa, the Tainui came to Tamaki, where the wanderers landed. They went up the river until they came to the portage that lies between the harbours of Waitemata and Manukau. There they saw seagulls and oyster-catchers flying overhead from the west, and guessed that the ocean on the other side of the land could not be far away. In the distance their scouts saw the silvery gleam of the Manukau Harbour and they decided to drag the canoe overland at Otahuhu and launch her again on the western shore.

Other canoes had come to Tamaki. Tokomaru crossed the island first, but Tainui soon followed. Turning southwards, this canoe finally reached Kawhia where it was beached and later buried. The head and stern-pieces, turned to stone, can be seen projecting above the ground to this day.

A less fortunate end awaited Te Arawa. She was burnt by Raumati of the Tainui tribe, thus causing endless strife between the two peoples. The descendants of Tainui settled in the Waikato and were neighbours of the Arawa tribes at Rotorua and the Bay of Plenty.

The Kurahaupo made
ready for sea

The Mataatua (though some traditions say it was the Aotea) was made of one half of a tree that fell and split into two pieces and was made into two canoes. Kura-aura, her captain, brought her to her final resting place at Whakatane.

The Tokomaru arrived at the east coast, rounded the North Cape, and sailed down the west coast as far as the Mohakatino River. The anchor of the canoe was kept there for hundreds of years until at last it found a home in the New Plymouth Museum.

The descendants of Tokomaru spread northward to the Mokau River and formed the southern boundary of Tainui.

Little is known of the Kurahaupo. The Nga-puhi of the north say that it was petrified into a reef on the east coast, but the people of Aotea say that it was wrecked at some time on the journey, and that the occupants were transferred to their canoe.

The shipwreck was supposed to have taken place in the Kermadec Islands. If that is so it explains why the Kurahaupo people became scattered, for it is possible that some came on in the Aotea while the Kurahaupo was repaired and brought to Aotearoa by the remainder of the crew. One group of descendants inhabited the parts where the canoe was supposed to have been petrified on the east coast of the Auckland Peninsula. A second group inhabited the country between the borders of Tainui and Aotea. Mount Egmont lies in this region, and its Maori name, Taranaki, is a tribal name of Kurahaupo.

Yet another group settled further south and occupied the land from Whangaehu to Horowhenua. They claim that Ruatea, the commander of Kurahaupo, was their ancestor.

The Kurahaupo is wrecked

25

# Aotea, Takitimu, and Horouta Canoes

Of the canoes that did not accompany the Great Fleet but sailed about the same time, the Aotea, commanded by Turi, sailed from Ra'iatea. She was beached at Rangi-tahua (Sunday Island) where she was refitted during the journey. Ririno also sailed with Turi, but they quarrelled over Kupe's sailing directions and parted company. Some say that Ririno was lost, others that he was wrecked on Boulder Bank near Nelson.

The Aotea gave its name to a small harbour on the west coast of the North Island where the canoe first landed. She was abandoned there, Turi and his men following the coastline by land until they reached the Patea River, where they settled. Their descendants made their way up the Whanganui River. Turi was the great name-giver of Taranaki. He brought many valuable plants with him, and his canoe has been known as Aotea the Richly Laden.

Five canoes sailed under the command of Tamatea, but only two survived, the Takitimu, and the Horouta which joined her sister vessel at Rarotonga. Takitimu was the first arrival. She landed near North Cape, but a heavy storm arose and she put to sea again. Tamatea and his people stayed for several years at Hokianga, but later Takitimu rounded North Cape and sailed on to Whakatane. A pa was built and a number of the crew settled there. Tamatea took the canoe back to the Bay of Islands where about a quarter of his followers decided to remain. Setting out again, he came to Waiapu on the east coast, where he found some of the men and women who had sailed in the Horouta. Still more of his people were left at Waiapu, but the restless Tamatea pushed off, taking some of the Ngati-Waitaha people with him. They visited the South Island, and tradition says that Takitimu was petrified into a range of mountains in Otago that still bears its name.

And so the new country was settled. Descendants of the Arawa and Mataatua voyagers set up their homes in different parts of the Bay of Plenty; those of Tainui in the Waikato; while the descendants of the pioneering Takitimu and Horouta sailors are to be found in the East Coast and East Cape districts. In this way Aotearoa was divided roughly into canoe districts.

There are many other stories told of those early days of settlement; they can be found in the great tribal histories that some day you may be glad to read. The events that have been related in this little book are just part of the story of the coming of the Maori to Aotearoa. It is simply legend, but legend that is a part of the history that has come to us through the unwritten pages of legend and song.

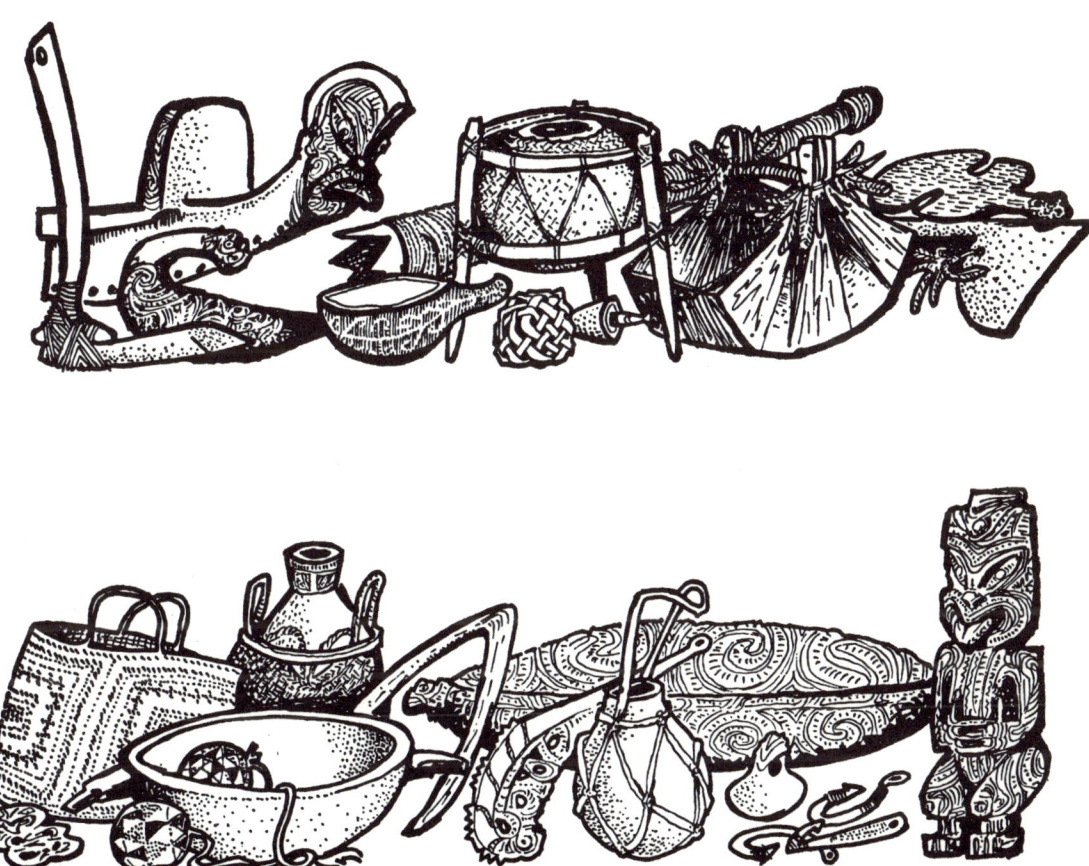

As the years and centuries passed by the descendants of the pioneer settlers developed their own tools, weapons, artifacts, and forms of art. This picture shows some of these interesting and valuable objects.

By permission of the Lands and Survey Department.

The location of the principal tribes of New Zealand about 1800. "Ngati-Akarana" and "Ngati-Poneke" are modern names and have no historical significance. Te Arawa is a confederation of tribes.

## Chapter Two   HOW THE MAORIS LIVED

The Maoris settled in all parts of New Zealand and built their villages or fortified pas near good hunting and fishing grounds. The pa was often placed on the top of a small hill where it could easily be defended. A narrow path wound up the hill, and the pa was protected by tall, wooden fences and wide ditches. At the corners were high towers, where sentries kept watch for enemies.

The houses were inside the fences. They were called whares. There were no streets such as we have, but there was a wide, open space, known as the marae, where everyone gathered to hear the news, to listen to speeches, and to play.

Everyone was busy, even when the chief and his men were away fighting their enemies. The married women (whom you could tell by their tattooed chins and lips) squatted down to weave cloaks and mats; the girls performed their beautiful poi dances, while the boys practised hakas. Some of the old men polished green-stone adzes as they sat in the bright sunshine, and the women, helped by the slaves, prepared food for the evening meal.

# A Maori Village

There were two kinds of whares in the Maori pa. Most of them were quite small and were more like huts. The larger whares were used for a number of purposes. The chiefs lived in special houses and there were others for entertaining important visitors. On wet days and in the evenings, people gathered in a large whare for singing, dancing or speech-making.

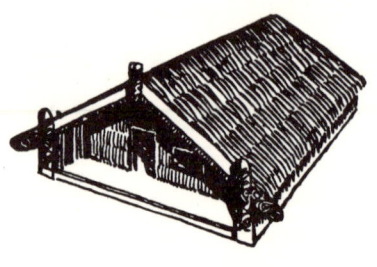

All the whares had thatched roofs, and the larger ones had wonderful carving in front and on panels inside the houses. The rafters were painted in patterns of white, red, and brown, and the sides of the house were decorated with coloured reeds, woven in different designs. At the front of the house there was a verandah where people could shelter from the sun or the rain during the day, a sliding wooden window, and a door in the front wall of the whare.

The small huts were only about four metres long, and were much plainer than the larger whares, and usually without a verandah. There was little or no carving in them. Soon we will go right inside one of the bigger houses and find out what it is like to live in a Maori whare.

But first let us look at it from the outside. See how well it is made. The thatched roof keeps out the rain and the little carved figure on the gable in front seems to keep watch. It took the best workmen of the tribe a long time to build this house, and to carve the lovely patterns in wood with their stone and greenstone tools.

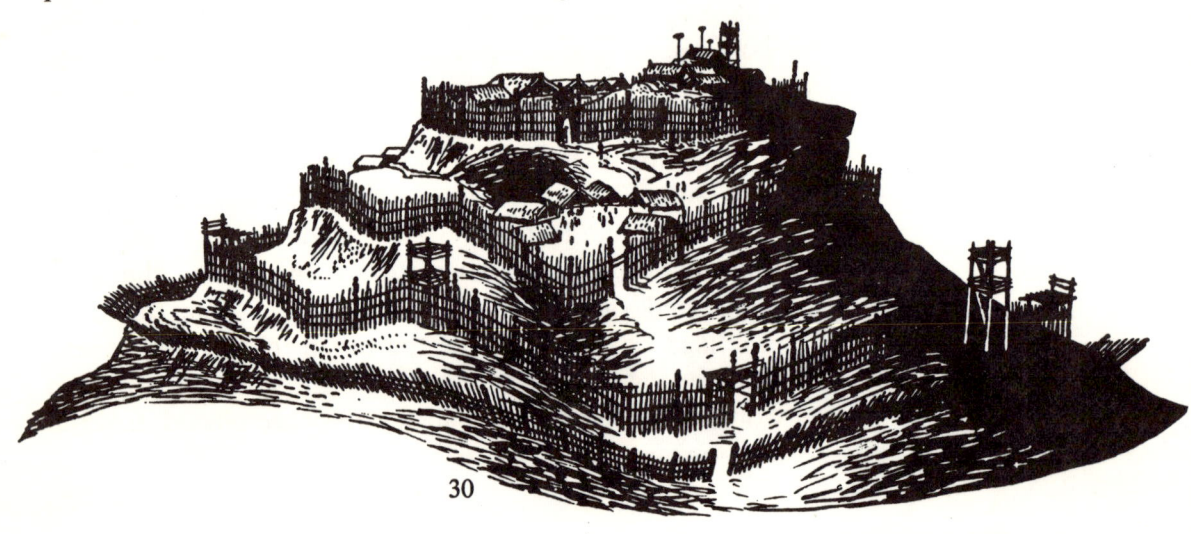

# The Maori at Home

The whare had no furniture, not even beds to sleep on, and very little air or light. Meals were always eaten outside the house, because food destroyed the tapu, or sacredness, and could not be brought indoors.

The Maoris slept on flax mats spread over fern leaves or brushwood. Along the sides of the whare the roof came close to the ground, but there was enough room to lie down. In cold weather a fire burned in a hollow in the earth floor, but there was no chimney for the smoke. Sometimes there was a hole in the roof, and the smoke filled the house and seeped out at the top.

The big House of Games would often be filled with people, and it grew very hot, especially in winter time, when the fires were burning. If anyone went outside, his almost-naked body would steam in the cold air

31

after being in the house. Sometimes people died because of the fumes of the fire, and then the Maoris thought that they had been killed by evil spirits.

There was great fun in the whare at night, especially when visitors were there. The children loved to sit up and see what was happening. The chiefs strode up and down as they made their speeches. Then the songs and dances began. The flickering light from the fires shone on the limbs and bodies of the dancers. As the young women of the tribe sang and swayed gracefully in time with the music, their poi-balls made of flax and filled with raupo-down, fluttered in their hands like fantails. Then an old chieftainess with crinkled face, with her chin and lips tattooed blue, told a story, and everyone laughed and shouted for more.

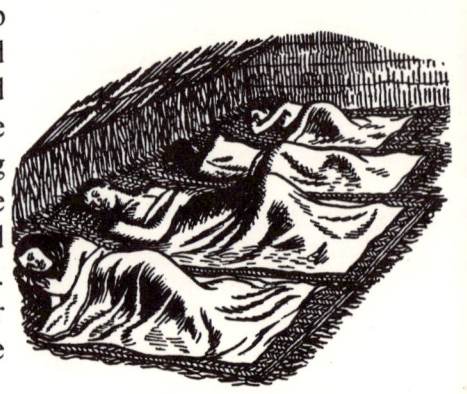

It was late when the children lay down to sleep, but no one minded, because Maori people always spoiled them a little.

## How They Lived Together

There were uncles and aunts, great-uncles and great-aunts, and grandparents in one big family. All the people who were related to each other were known as the whanau, or family group. The older folk were fond of the children, who called them all "father" or "mother". If a Maori boy was speaking of his own mother he would call her his "true" mother.

The people in the whanau decided all family matters themselves, even whom the young people should marry! The families belonged to part of the tribe called the hapu. The tribe, which was called the iwi, was made up of many hapus. The ruler of the iwi was the ariki, who was very powerful in time of war, but who usually talked with other chiefs and leading people in the tribe before deciding on anything that was important.

After the ariki came the rangatiras. Nearly everyone called himself a rangatira, or free man, and was proud that he was not a slave or a common person. Prisoners who were captured in war were made slaves, and had to wait on their masters.

Sometimes they were in danger of being knocked on the head with a club and cooked in the oven if things went wrong; but often they were well-treated and had a happy time in the family group.

No wonder the boys and girls were sometimes spoiled, seeing that they had so many mothers and fathers! They were able to run about and do as they liked, and there were no lessons for young children, except the important ones of copying mother and father and learning to grow up into brave men and women.

## The Clothes They Wore

When the children were small, they didn't have to bother with clothes. In the daytime they were always warm because they were running about. When the weather was cold, the sleeping house was warm. In some parts of New Zealand there were hot pools where they could swim or play or lie in the water for hours, listening to the old people telling stories.

33

As they grew up, they began to wear clothes like the older people. There were only two garments. Men wore the same kind of clothes as women. There was a kilt or skirt fastened by a belt, and a cloak, which was a square of woven flax, tied across the shoulders. The cloak was not usually worn when working. The Maoris went barefoot, and did not wear hats, although ranga-tiras were proud to wear a huia feather in their hair.

The garments were woven by the women-folk, but their method of weaving was very slow. The women placed two or four sticks upright in the ground, and tied a piece of flax between them. Other lengths of flax were tied to this string, and pieces of flax woven in and out of the hanging threads. It took months to make a cloak, but the finished garment was often beautiful because some of the threads were dyed red or black, and woven into patterns. The most valuable cloaks were decorated with kiwi feathers or tufts of dog's hair.

Perhaps you are wondering what men did for pockets. Both men and women used baskets for carrying things in, but the men often wore their belts folded over, and used the fold for carrying little articles.

It did not take people long to get dressed in those days, but they had ornaments as well as clothes. There were greenstone ear-pendants, tikis to hang round their necks, and necklaces of shark's teeth. Most important of all was the moko. This was the tattooed pattern which was carved on their faces and bodies and limbs.

34

# How Food Was Grown

The kumara, or sweet potato, was the most important crop. The different sections of the tribe each brought one seed-kumara from their store, and these offerings were planted by the tohungas, who prayed to the Kumara God to give them a good crop.

When this was done, the men took their digging sticks and, standing in rows, they pressed the points of their sticks into the ground and turned over a long sod of earth. As they worked they sang an old song together to make the work less tiring. When the ground was turned over, the women followed, breaking up the earth with wooden clubs, and picking out all the roots.

Women were not allowed to plant the seed-kumaras. This was a sacred task which could only be done by the men. The women were allowed to keep the weeds down and pick off the caterpillars as the crops were growing. The kumara patch was a sacred place where strangers did not dare to go. There were no wild animals to be kept out, although the hungry swamp-hen sometimes made a raid.

Clearing the ground for kumara (from the drawing by de Sainson, 1827, in D'Urville's *Voyage Pittoresque*).

When the crop was fully grown and the kumaras gathered, they were stored in pits. The people were often hungry at this time of the year, and a great feast was held. They did not forget the gods who had been kind to them, and a special oven was made for Rongo and Pani, who had watched over their crops.

Other good crops were the yam, the taro, and the hue, or gourd plant, which also provided bowls and jars. These were very useful, because the Maori had not found out how to make pots from clay. If the kumara crop failed, and food was short, the people would have to eat tasteless food such as pounded fern-root made into cakes.

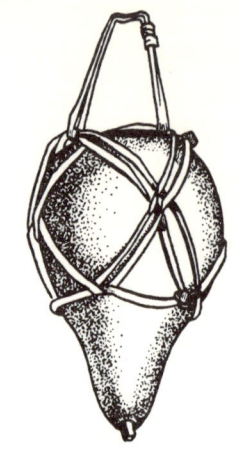

Calabash made from a gourd.

Rua, or underground storehouse for root crops.

## How They Hunted Birds

Taro

Although the men left the weeding of the vegetable patch to the women, they would not allow them to take part in hunting.

The forests were the home of the birds, and they were carefully looked after by the hunters. The Maoris had many charms to stop the birds from flying away, and to attract them to their hunting-grounds.

The hunters had many different kinds of snares. There were snares to set on the little forest paths for rats and flightless birds like the kiwi; there were snares that were put round water troughs to catch pigeons and other birds when they came to drink; and there were snares that were set far out on the ends of branches, so that only the most daring hunters could reach them.

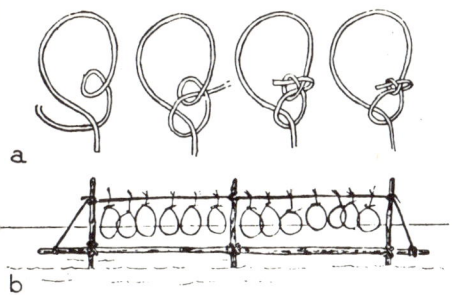

a. Noose snare (after Best). b. Snares above water (after Buck).

Some trees which bore a big crop of berries were favourite perching places for the birds. The hunters knew all about these trees. They built platforms in the branches, and lay in wait, armed with long wooden spears which were sometimes ten metres in length. When a plump bird alighted on a twig, the hunter pushed his spear slowly and carefully through the leaves and then, with one quick thrust, he speared the unlucky bird.

The noisy kakas were so strong that they broke the snares. The hunters speared them, or caught them in their hands, and sometimes on cold, frosty nights tuis were caught in the same way, because they were so cold that they could not fly away.

When the hunters examined their snares they were careful not to say anything the forest birds might overhear, in case they should be frightened. The bird hunters were very clever people, for the whole tribe depended on them for food.

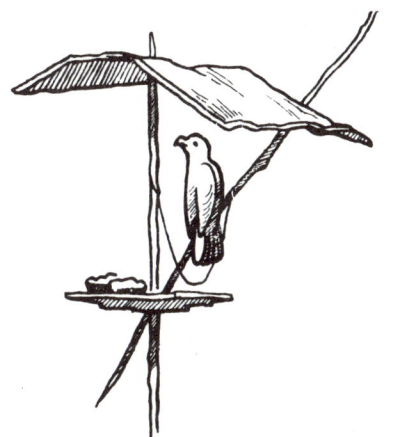

Domesticated kaka parrot used as a decoy (after Angas).

Barbed bird spear point.

Snaring the woodhen.

# How They Caught Fish

Mode of fishing with nets on Lake Taupo (after Angas).

The tribes which lived by the seaside had plenty of fish to eat; others lived by the lakes; and all the inland tribes were able to catch eels in the rivers and streams.

They built weirs with nets where they caught the eels as they made their way down to the sea. The eels were also caught with spears or by hand. Maori boys sometimes dived into a pool, and when they had caught a slippery eel, held it in their teeth to prevent it escaping as they swam ashore. The tiny whitebait, too, were a real titbit for the river-fishers.

The Maori was a good fisherman. He had many different nets, from small handnets used by one man, to the seine nets nearly 1,000 metres long. A large flax net would be made by several villages, and they shared in its use. The first time the net was used was a great occasion, for many spells and incantations were repeated, and gifts were made to the sea-gods.

Fishing grounds were chosen for each tribe. Big canoes were used by the Maori fishermen. They often went many miles out to sea. Food was not allowed on these canoes, and the tohunga, who was a fishing expert as well as a priest, recited charms to make the fishing successful. The lines were made of flax, and the hooks of wood or bone, often elaborately carved, and made in many different sizes for different kinds of fish. Sharks were prized for their oil as well as for their flesh, and the teeth were used for necklaces.

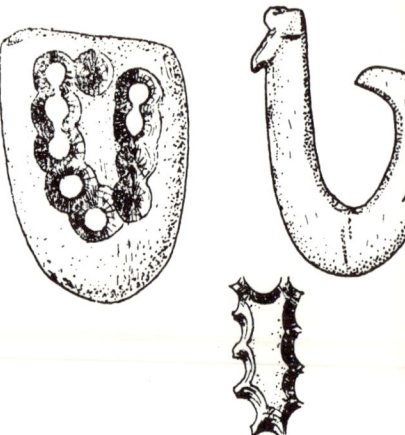

Making a fish hook.

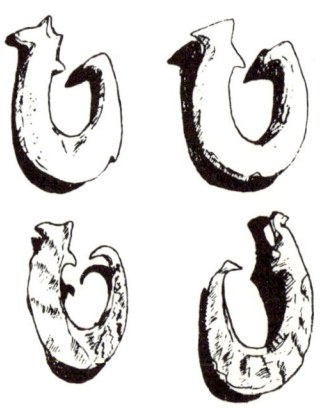

Shell hooks (matau), Hawke's Bay.

38

We must not forget the shellfish – the pipis and mussels and toheroas which were gathered from the beaches or dug up from the sand and mud at low tide. We still find huge heaps of shells that remind us of the millions of shellfish which were eaten by the Maoris in bygone days.

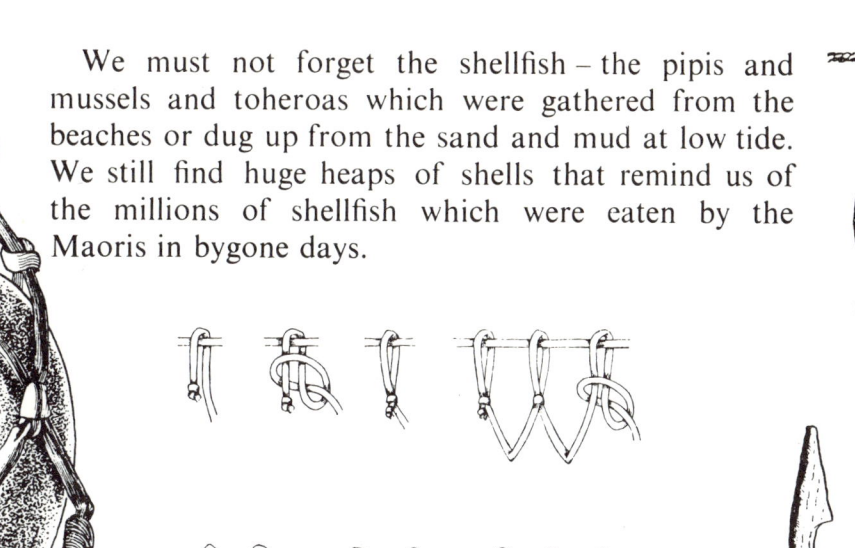

nclosed stone sinker.

Maori netting (after Sir Peter Buck).

Hook with wooden shank.

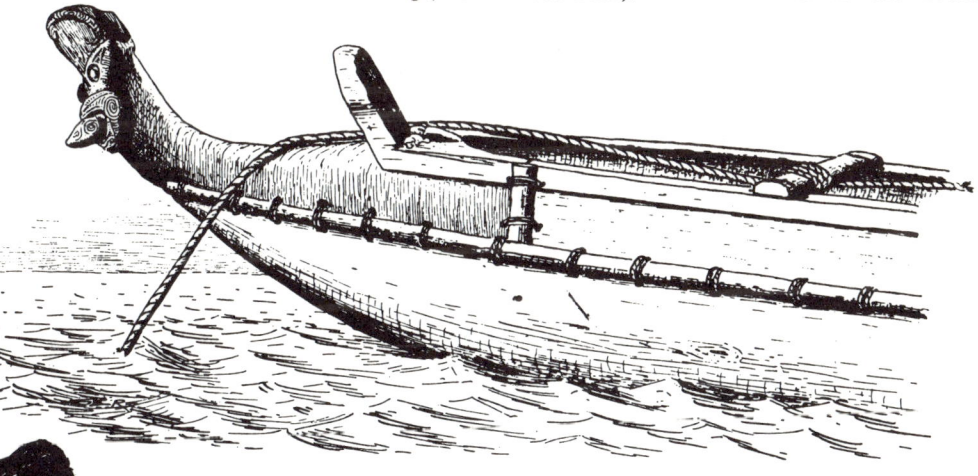

Fishing canoe prow, illustrating method of anchoring.

# How They Cooked Their Food

We have seen how the Maori gathered his food from the forest and the sea and from his gardens. To these foods he added berries, and dainty morsels such as rats, which were caught in snares. Sometimes food was scarce and he had to work very hard to keep from starving. It is no wonder that in times of plenty he had great feasts and ate far more than a white man

Fire making.

could. He always shared his food gladly with visitors, and sometimes he entertained them so well that he went hungry for months afterwards.

Cooking was left to the women, who made tempting meals with the stores of kumaras, fresh food and dried fish, and the birds, which were preserved in fat. Let us see them as they set to work. Holes were dug in the ground. Great fires were lit in these holes and stones laid on top. As the wood burned away the stones became red-hot. Leaves and branches were laid on the hot stones, and the food was placed on top. Another layer of leaves was then put over the food. Water was sprinkled over the leaves, which were covered with flax mats, and then earth was heaped over and stamped flat. The steam from the water and the hot stones cooked the food. When the oven was opened about two hours later, the food was taken out steaming hot and beautifully cooked.

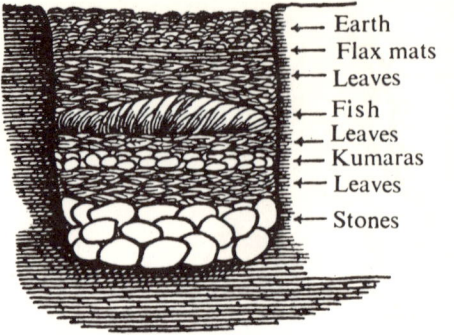

— Earth
— Flax mats
— Leaves
— Fish
— Leaves
— Kumaras
— Leaves
— Stones

All the cooking was done out of doors, but sheds were built for use in wet weather. These were cold, cheerless places, because they were really only roofs supported on posts. Food, especially cooked food, destroyed tapu, and could not be taken inside the whares, so the women had to work outside in the cold.

There were no plates or pots of any kind, except an occasional gourd which contained water into which hot stones were dropped to heat it. Shallow flax baskets or plates were woven to hold food, and these were made very quickly by the women and used as dishes.

Flax basket and gourds.

## The Games They Played

The Maoris could not read, but there was always much to keep them busy. There were plenty of games to play at night and on wet days. First of all, there was music and dancing, but we will read about these later.

Cat's-cradle was a popular game with young and old, and was called whai. A long piece of flax cord was used, and many of the designs were very complicated. The players often had to use their teeth and their toes as well as hands. Sometimes several players joined together to make difficult designs which were supposed to be pictures of some of the old legends.

Top-spinning was played by men and boys. They had both whip tops and humming tops. The whip tops were "whipped" over little ridges of earth. Humming tops were sometimes used by the old people when they were mourning for a dead friend.

Many of the games needed skill. Ti rakau, or stick tossing, was one of these. The players squatted in a circle, holding short sticks in their hands. They all sang a song, and at certain words in the song they tossed their sticks from one to another in time with the music.

The older people joined the children in many of the games, or played by themselves. Many of their games were played seriously, because they helped to train their bodies and their minds. It was important that everyone should have a good memory, because there were no books to record important matters like family trees, sacred spells and incantations, which every Maori had to learn.

## Outdoor Sports

The days passed quickly because there were so many exciting games to play. There were simple games like tree-climbing, swimming, running, sliding downhill on a leaf of the nikau palm, or swinging on trailing lengths of supplejack in the forest.

Down by the river or the pool, there was usually a moari, which was a tall pole with ropes hanging from the top. The players swung round at the end of the ropes and then dropped feet first into the water. Everyone joined in this exciting game.

There were stilts, and the boys became very clever at walking on them. They held stilt races, and even wrestled and crossed rivers on them.

Kite-flying was a very popular sport with older people as well as with the children. The kites were covered with a light material woven from the bark of the aute tree, and often made in the shape of a bird, so they were called manu, which means bird. The younger children had just as much fun with their light raupo or reed kites.

Games are often a form of training for something in later life, and many of the sports were a preparation for the fighting that Maori boys looked forward to when they grew up. The games that were played with weapons were the most important of all. The boys and young men fought with light reeds, which did not hurt, but prepared them for the use of the fighting taiaha, which we shall read about later. They learned to defend themselves by parrying the blows, or dodging them by jumping from side to side.

In another game, darts made of light reeds were thrown against a low mound so that they glided off, and contests were held to see who could throw his dart the furthest. Spears were thrown with a whip, and slings were also used.

All kinds of races were popular, especially canoe-racing and swimming. The Maoris loved the water, and could swim almost like fish, so they never minded if their light, one-man canoes were upset. At the seaside, surf-riding in small canoes or on boards was always popular.

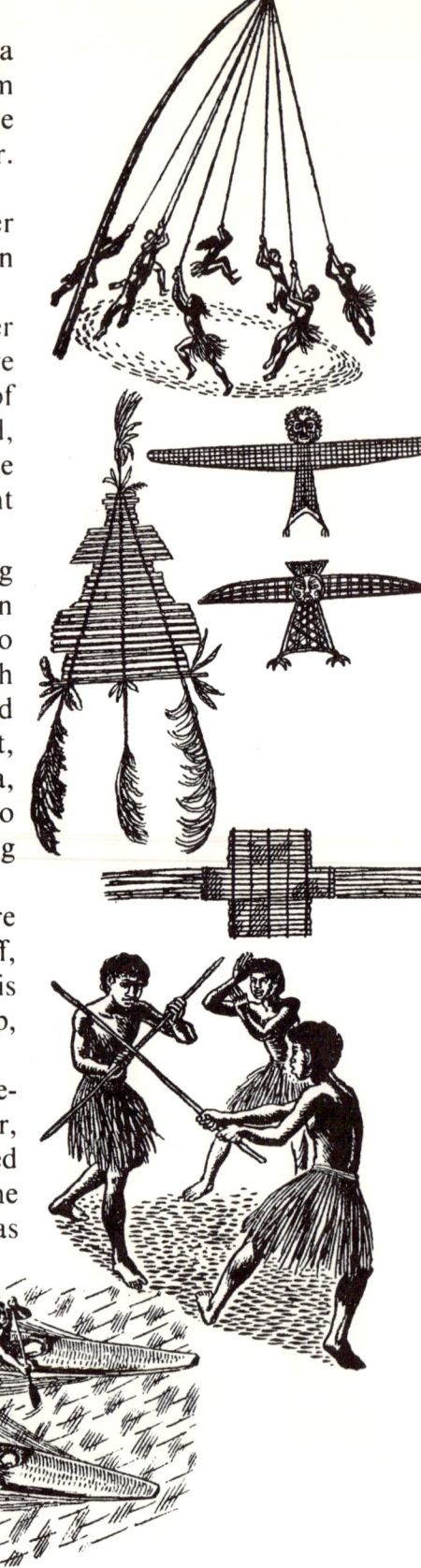

# Music and Dances

Singing was more important to the Maoris than it is to us. They had no written language, and legends and history were remembered because of the songs that were sung about them. Visitors were greeted with songs. The dead were farewelled with songs, and the Maori was always ready to show his feelings in this way. Men and women often broke into song in the middle of a speech, and the song was just as important as the speech itself. There were few musical instruments. Flutes were usually made of wood and elaborately carved, though sometimes they were made from one of the bones of a dead enemy! One kind of flute was played by blowing into it through the nostril. There were also several kinds of trumpets, which were used for signalling in time of war. There were no stringed instruments of any kind.

The best time to listen to the singing was at night in the whare, when all the people were sitting together in the firelight, joining in the old songs, and watching the women and girls perform the poi or ball dance. The pois were like soft balls stuffed with the down of the raupo, and fastened to a flax cord. As they danced, the women sang and the pois fluttered in their hands in time with the music. These poi dances imitated common actions such as paddling and tree-felling.

The haka was a frightening performance. It was a dance in which arms, legs and bodies all took part with fierce stamping of the feet, rolling eyeballs, horrible faces and protruding tongues, but it was often a dance of welcome to visitors. Men and women both took part in it. The haka was also a war dance, and we will read about it on the next page.

Flutes.

43

# *Warfare*

The grown-up men spent a great deal of their time in fighting. When a war-party or taua went out to fight, it was under the protection of a god, and all the warriors had to be careful what they did, lest they should offend the god and be wounded or killed. A tohunga always went with the taua to chant the right spells and incantations. The first person to be met by a war party on its way to fight, whether friend or enemy, was killed and offered to the gods.

Unless the taua was making a surprise attack, the haka was danced by the two fighting parties. It was a fearsome sight, as each tribe did its best to frighten the enemy. The ground shook with the weight of the warriors as they stamped the earth and shouted their blood-curdling war-cries.

The Maori's only throwing weapon was the spear. Most of the fights were hand-to-hand, fought with light, but carefully made weapons, which were often treasured heirlooms. The principal weapons were the taiaha, the tewhatewha, and the mere or patu.

Canoes on a raiding expedition (early Missionary publication).

Taiahas.

The taiaha was a kind of spear, made of manuka, very light and strong. It had a carved tongue at one end, which was used as a striking point. The handle was flattened, and the butt end was used like a club, the end being brought over to give a stunning blow to an enemy. The tewhatewha was more like a battle-axe, but was made of wood.

The patu weapons were really clubs, and were made of hard wood, stone, bone, or greenstone. They were broad and flat, with a fairly sharp edge, and were the favourite weapons for in-fighting. The mere-pounamu (greenstone club) was the most prized weapon that the Maori possessed.

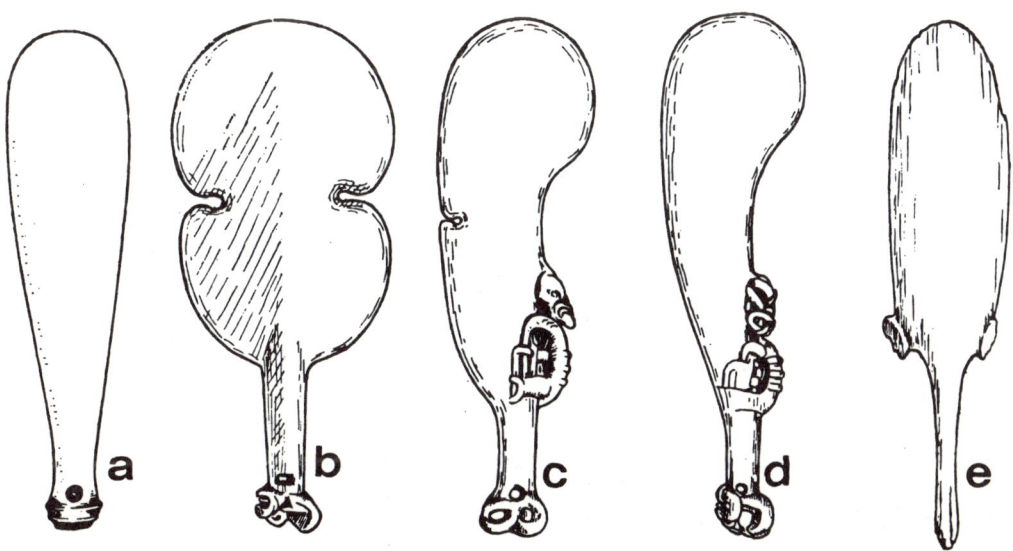

Short weapons: a. patu onewa; b. kotiate; c. wahaika; d. wahaika; e. shouldered patu, Otago. (After Skinner).

45

# How Carving Was Done

We have seen that the Maori was very fond of carving. He carved houses, canoes, weapons, tools, and even his own skin. Let us look more closely at this wonderful art.

It is not really sculpture, is it? There are some races of people who try to draw pictures of what they see, or to make models of them, but the Maori preferred to make designs. He carved spirals, the ends of which are difficult to find, so carefully are they drawn. He carved the hard boards of the canoe stern pieces into something which looked like delicate lace. On his houses there were strange pictures of men with long tongues and staring eyes made of paua shell, and with hands with only three fingers.

It is wonderful to think that all this lovely, delicate carving was done with greenstone chisels, which had to be ground and polished for months or years before they were ready for use. Greenstone was one of the most treasured possessions of the Maori. It was hard, and took a good cutting edge, so that it was used for making axes and fighting weapons.

The carving on their faces and bodies was as wonderful as the carving in wood. The same sort of patterns were used. Tattooing was called moko, and was painful and dangerous. The lines were marked out in charcoal, and then the grooves were made with a sharp-edged chisel, which was tapped against the skin. The tattooing expert kept wiping the blood away as he carved his design. Only a little could be done at a time, because the skin became swollen and sore.

Special tohungas, or experts, were employed in carving and tattooing, and they received valuable gifts in payment for their work.

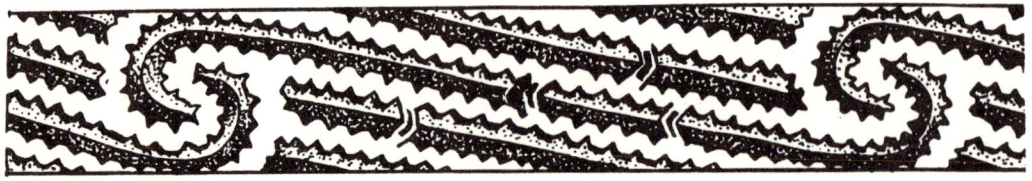

46

# What the Maoris Believed

It is just as important for us to know what people think as to know what they do. Most of the things they do come from what they think. We cannot really understand "the old-time Maori," but we know some of the things he thought about, which help us to learn some important things.

He was a brave fighter, generous to his friends, and fond of children. He had no real home life as we do, but thought of the tribe as his family. He followed his ariki in time of war, and was always careful not to offend the gods. The tohungas, who were trained in special schools, told him about the gods, and what different omens meant, and what was tapu. This is a word which we must remember, because it was very important. Tapu means sacred, or forbidden. Some things were sacred, and no Maori ever dared touch them. A chief's head was tapu, and the tribal burial ground was tapu. Sometimes a precious ornament could be made tapu, so that no one could take it.

Some of the tohungas or priests believed in Io, the God who could not be seen, or even imagined. He was the Creator. Io was known only to a few tohungas, but everyone knew about the famous gods of war and peace, of forest and sea, of wind and cultivated food, of sky and earth. There were many stories about the world when it was young. Tane, the god of nature, separated the Sky Father and Earth Mother so that light could come in, and man could live on the earth. Then there were the gods of the rainbow and the mist, and wandering spirits who were found everywhere. It was just as well to keep indoors at night, because of the fairy men of the forest, and the ghosts of ancestors, who could only be kept away by the sacred red ochre and the right spells.

This was the Maori as he lived in the fair land of Aotearoa many, many years ago. He had his happy times, but there were some things which made him unhappy, just as we have good and bad things in our lives.

*Chapter Three* **HOW NEW ZEALAND WAS REDISCOVERED**

The Polynesian explorers and sailors were the first discoverers of New Zealand. We should remember with pride the discoveries of Maui the mythical fisherman; Kupe and Ngahue who found greenstone, hunted the moa, and returned to their homeland to tell the tale of their adventures; Whatonga and his grandfather Toi, who were the first settlers whose names have been preserved in legend; the commanders of the canoes of the Fleet—Tama-te-kapua, captain of the Arawa and the tohunga Ngatoro-i-rangi, Turi of the Aotea, Hoturoa of the Tainui, and many others. And then there were the thousands of nameless pioneers—the Moa-hunters and the Polynesians who came from tropic islands to these green islands in the South Pacific.

The centuries passed slowly by. The descendants of the first settlers grew in number. As we have seen, they made their homes in different parts of the country. They were proud of their ancestors as we, too, should be. They never dreamed that there were white people in other parts of the world, far distant from their own Hawaiki, the homeland of the race. They worked in their plantations, hunted birds and rats in the forest, fished in lakes, rivers, and sea, danced and sang·on the marae and in the big meeting-houses, and waged war against their enemies.

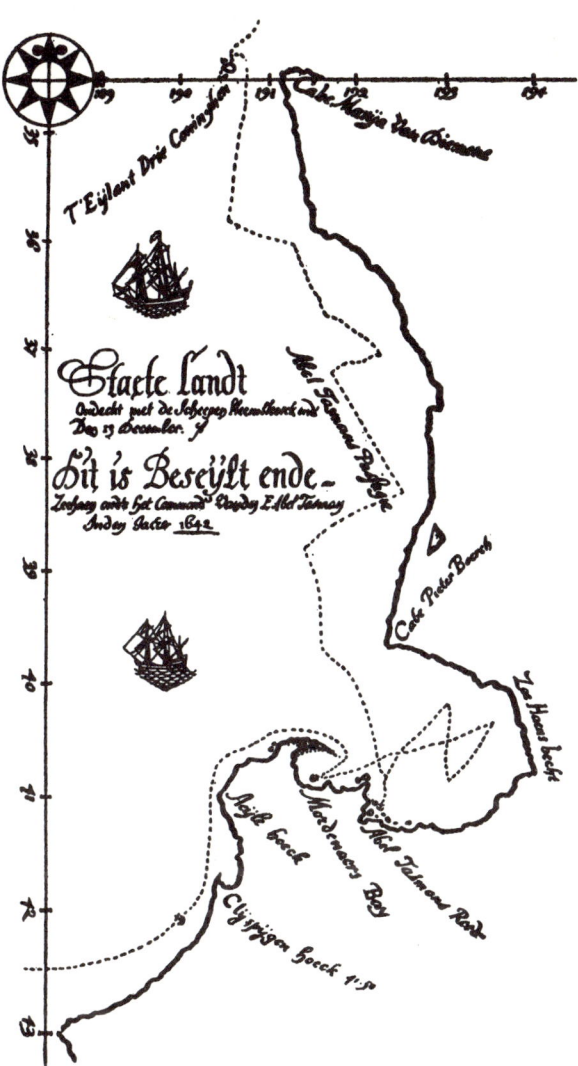

Abel Tasman's Chart of New
Zealand, then known as Staten Land.

Abel Janszoon Tasman.

# Abel Tasman

On the opposite side of the world, in Europe, there was also warfare between one country and another. The population of the Old World was increasing. As larger ships were built and the art of navigation improved, men began to explore the oceans of the then unknown world. Christopher Columbus discovered America, Francis Drake sailed right round the world, and other seafarers looked for new lands where their countrymen could found colonies and bring back gold and other precious commodities to their own land. Presently the exploring ships began to enter the Pacific Ocean.

Amongst the most adventurous explorers were the people of Holland. They were good businessmen and traders as well as skilful navigators. They had travelled as far as the islands known as the Dutch East Indies which, in the twentieth century, have become independent and have been renamed Indonesia. The geographers of the seventeenth and eighteenth centuries believed that there must be a large continent somewhere in the South Seas, and many of the early explorers travelled long distances through perilous uncharted oceans in search of this fabulous land.

In the year 1642 Abel Janszoon Tasman, a Dutch commander, set out from Batavia (now Djakarta) on the island of Java, with two ships, the *Heemskirk* and the *Zeehaen*. After calling at Mauritius he sailed eastwards for many weeks until he came to a large island which he called Van Diemen's Land for the Governor-General of Batavia. Many years afterwards it was renamed Tasmania in honour of the explorer.

Tasman kept sailing towards the south-east until one day he came in sight of the snow-covered ranges of the South Island of New Zealand. This was the first time

they had been seen by a European. Thirteenth December 1642 will always be an important date for New Zealanders to remember, because on that day Tasman wrote in his log "Toward noon we saw a large, high-lying land bearing South-east of us."

The two ships sailed up the east coast. Although they kept as close to the rocky coast as they dared, there was no sign of life on shore. At length they rounded Cape Farewell and dropped anchor in the calm waters of a large bay. Several canoes were seen. The Dutchmen tried to attract the Maoris to the ships by holding up cloth and knives, but the men in the canoes were suspicious, and would not come any closer.

After spending some time at anchor, the captain of the *Zeehaen* went across to the *Heemskirk* with some of his men in a small boat. Before it could reach the mother ship it was rammed by a canoe and several of the crew were killed. Abel Tasman and his officers then decided it would be dangerous to go ashore amongst such a warlike people.

The anchors were raised and the ships sailed away. The Dutchmen suspected that the land might be an island, and that they would be able to complete their journey by continuing eastward, but the winds were treacherous. After tacking to and fro for several days they abandoned the attempt and sailed northward. Tasman called a point of land Cape Maria Van Diemen after the wife of the governor of Batavia. When he came in sight of the Three Kings Islands he named them for the wise men or kings who worshipped the infant Christ, because these tiny islands were first seen on the day that is kept in memory of the three kings.

Hoping that the country he had discovered was part of the "Southern Continent", Tasman called it Staten land; but when Staten at the tip of Argentina in South

America was found to be an island, and not part of the fabulous continent, as most people thought, Tasman's land was renamed after the Dutch province of Zealand.

Although the explorer was disappointed, because he thought that his voyage had brought no results and because he had discovered no treasures, he had done far more than he imagined. The islands that are now known as New Zealand were at last on the map of the world, even though they were only represented by one wiggling line and a few names, of which only one remains on present day maps.

The memorial to the great Dutch explorer in the Abel Tasman National Park in the province of Nelson.

# James Cook

And that is what New Zealand looked like on maps for 127 years, until Captain Cook sailed into the Southern Ocean in the year 1769. James Cook was an officer in the British Navy. Because of his reputation as a careful navigator, he had been put in command of the tubby, blunt-nosed sailing ship, the bark *Endeavour*, to convey scientists to the other side of the world where they were to make observations of the planet Venus as it passed across the face of the sun.

Lieutenant Cook, as he was then, made the long, dangerous voyage to Tahiti, which had been discovered only a few years before. The observations were successful. Cook then sailed south to see if he could find the legendary continent. Little did he know, as the ship drew away from the friendly islands of Tahiti, that he was following the long-vanished wake of Kupe and Toi and the commanders of the canoes of the great fleet.

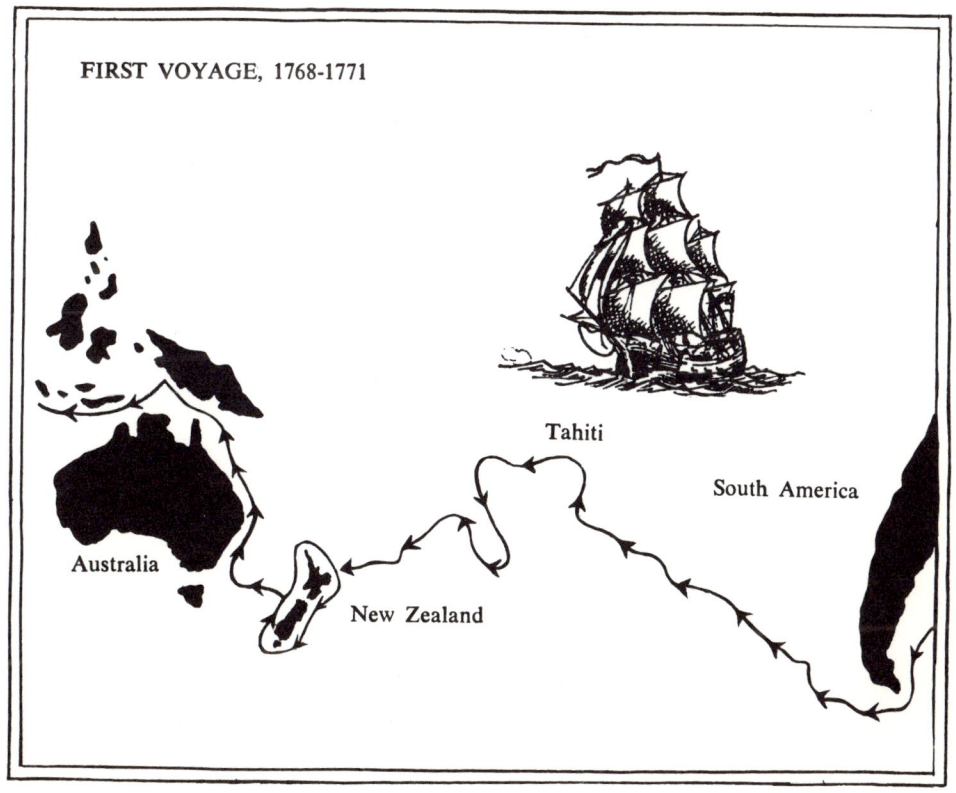

FIRST VOYAGE, 1768-1771

Tahiti

South America

Australia

New Zealand

CAPTAIN COOK

An engraving from an original picture
in the Gallery of Greenwich Hospital

Eventually the *Endeavour* made the same landfall. It was Nicholas Young, the surgeon's boy, who was the first to sight the coast of New Zealand on 7 October 1769.

"Land ho!" Nick shouted as he kept watch at the masthead. Cook was not surprised. All that day he had noticed that the sea was becoming lighter in colour. With his long experience he knew that it was a sign that the water was shoaling and that the ship must be getting close to land.

It was two o'clock in the afternoon when Nick made his discovery. By sunset the captain and the officers could see it plainly from the deck. With a twinkle in his eyes Cook decided to call the point of land Young Nick's Head.

The *Endeavour*

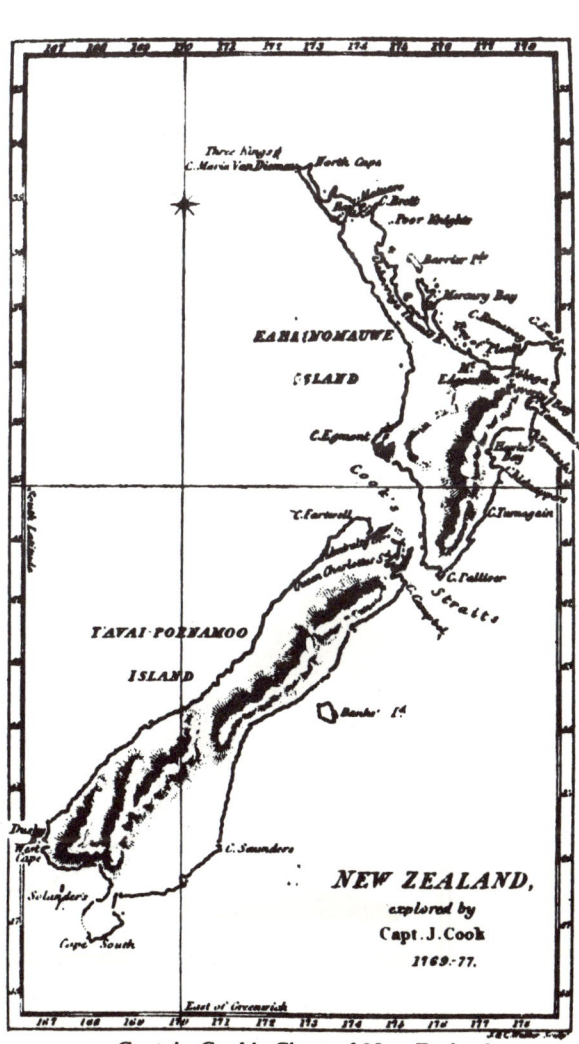

Captain Cook's Chart of New Zealand

It was the first place to be marked on a new chart that grew larger and more detailed as the weeks went by. Lieutenant Cook studied the secret instructions that had been given to him before he left England. He had been told to search for the Southern Continent "until you discover it or fall in with the eastern side of the land discovered by Tasman and now called New Zealand".

He had carried out his orders faithfully. As he sailed round the two islands it was interesting to see how Tasman's ragged line fitted into his accurately drawn chart. Notable as the Dutch captain's achievement had been, Cook's rediscovery and his plotting of the country was really far more important.

He charted the whole coast line, though he was not quite sure of Banks Peninsula and Stewart Island. He showed the main mountain ranges, gave names to all the prominent features, and landed at many places on the coast. More important, he made friends with the Maori people, and wrote a great deal about their manners and customs in his journal. He planted the Union Jack on an island in Queen Charlotte Sound, claiming the islands as a British possession, spent several months exploring the land, letting his men rest after their arduous voyage, and in later years he paid two further visits.

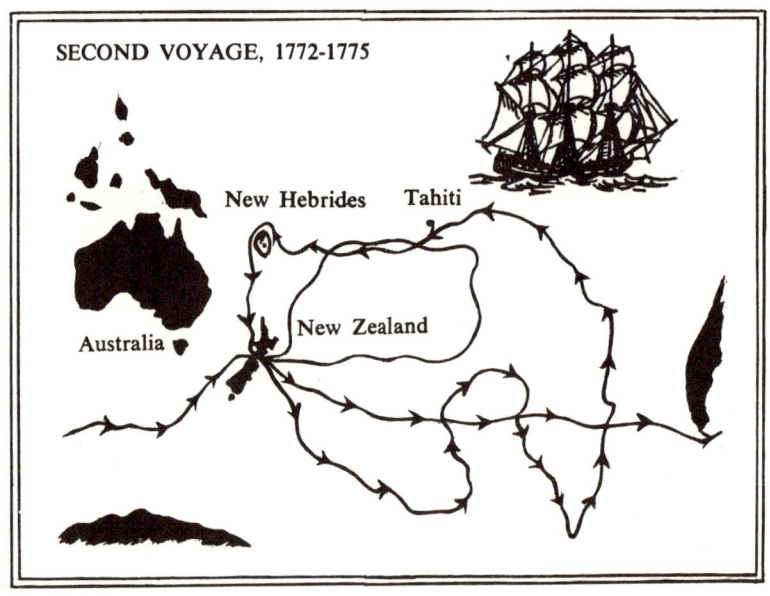

SECOND VOYAGE, 1772-1775

New Hebrides    Tahiti

Australia    New Zealand

# French Explorers

Shortly after the *Endeavour* reached New Zealand a curious thing happened. While the bark was driven away from land for a few days in December 1769 a French sloop, the *Saint Jean Baptiste*, commanded by Captain De Surville, came to anchor in Doubtless Bay. Captain Cook had taken great care of his sailors but De Surville, although a good seaman, was not nearly so concerned to see that his men kept in good health. Sixty of them had already died of scurvy, and the remainder of the crew were so feeble that they were scarcely able to row the ship's boats ashore. The Maoris were friendly, and a good supply of green vegetables soon cured the sick sailors.

The storm that kept the *Endeavour* at sea grew worse. The *Saint Jean Baptiste* was nearly wrecked. Three of the ship's boats had gone ashore, but only two of them were able to return. The sailors from the third boat were cared for by the Maoris. When they finally returned to the ship it was found that a dinghy had broken away during the storm and was being dragged into the bush by some of the Maoris. De Surville was a hot-tempered man. In spite of the kindness that the Maoris had shown to his sailors, he sent armed men ashore to burn canoes and houses and fishing nets, and captured one of the chiefs who had been kind to his sailors.

Shortly afterwards De Surville sailed away, taking his captive with him. The heart-broken chief died at sea. The vessel finally reached Peru, many thousands of kilometres away where the hard-hearted captain died. If only he had made friends with the Maoris he could have stayed in the shelter of the harbour and re-provisioned his ship. Then his name would have been remembered for his kindness as well as for his skill as a navigator.

Less than three years later another Frenchman arrived in New Zealand. By the time he left his home port, Captain Cook had returned to England from his first voyage, but Captain Marion du Fresne had not heard of his discoveries. After sighting Mount Egmont, which had been named by Cook, but had not been seen by Tasman because it was hidden in the clouds when he sailed past, the French ships *Mascarin* and *Marquis de Castries* sailed round North Cape and anchored in the Bay of Islands.

Captain du Fresne was not a cruel man like his fellow-countryman, De Surville. He pitched camp on the island of Moturua in the Bay so that some of his sick sailors could be looked after and made comfortable while others went over to the mainland to cut down trees for spars and firewood. Some of the officers warned the captain that the Maoris might prove treacherous, but Marion du Fresne replied, "How can you expect me to have a bad opinion of a people who show me so much friendship?"

Marion Du Fresne, at the Bay of Islands

Poor Marion! He was too trusting. It seems likely that the Maoris at the Bay of Islands had heard of De Surville's cruelty, and that they took their revenge on Captain du Fresne. While some of the sailors were working unsuspectingly in the bush, they were killed, and the captain was also put to death. The sailors who had remained on board the ships burned down a village, and then sailed away sadly without their commander. It was an unhappy ending for a man who in his own way had been as friendly to the Maoris as Captain Cook had been.

The death of Marion Du Fresne copied from a painting by the French artist Charles Meryon

## From 1773 to 1826

During the next fifty years many people arrived in New Zealand and added to the discoveries that had been made by the first British and French explorers. Sealers, whalers, traders, missionaries, escaped convicts from Australia, and pioneer settlers came to New Zealand. A midshipman named George Vancouver, who was on the *Resolution* during Cook's third visit, had risen to the rank of captain, and was placed in command of two vessels, the *Discovery* and the *Chatham*. In 1791 Vancouver set out on a voyage of exploration to the west coast of North America.

Leaving Van Diemen's Land (Tasmania) in October, he sailed across the Tasman Sea and entered the sound that Cook had named Dusky Bay. The ships stayed there for several weeks while Vancouver explored some of the inlets to the north of the sound. There was one inlet that Cook had not penetrated, and which he had named Nobody Knows What. Vancouver's men explored it, and the captain changed the name to Somebody Knows What. These names no longer appear on the map of New Zealand. The northern part of the inlet is now called Vancouver Arm and the southern part, Broughton Arm after the captain of the second vessel.

Vancouver and Broughton also discovered the Snares to the south of New Zealand, and later Captain Broughton landed on the Chatham Islands, which he named after his own vessel, and took possession of them.

A year or two later a Spanish expedition commanded by an Italian named Alessandro Malaspina spent some time in the sounds of Fiordland. It seems strange that a part of New Zealand that was practically unknown for more than 100 years afterwards should have been visited by people of so many different nationalities. The first sealing gang arrived there as early as 1792. Important discoveries were made in Foveaux Strait by an American, Owen F. Smith, who was able to correct Cook's chart and prove that Stewart Island was separated from the mainland. The island was not named until 1809 when Captain S. Chase sailed round it in the *Pegasus* and named it after his first mate. Captain Chase also proved that Banks Peninsula was part of the mainland, as Captain Cook had suspected.

Ships of several nations began to frequent the Bay of Islands before 1840, and gradually the blank spaces on Cook's chart were filled in. The most notable of these later explorers was Captain Dumont D'Urville, a man who was as modest and observant as Captain Cook.

*Dumont D'Urville*

Jules Sébastien César Dumont D'Urville was a French-man who was given command of the *Astrolabe* in 1826 to explore parts of the Pacific and to try to find out what had happened to another famous explorer, La Pérouse, who had been lost somewhere in the South Seas. His journals provide a great deal of information about the Maoris and other people whom he met on his voyages. Before he left France he secured a grammar of the Maori language that had been published a few years before, and was able to understand some of the things that the Maoris said, and to record names with some accuracy.

His first landfall was on the west coast of the South Island. He decided to explore the parts of the coast that Cook had not had time to examine. He had the advantage of being able to study the chart that Cook had prepared. He rounded Cape Farewell and sailed into Tasman Bay where Abel Tasman had made his only contact with the Maoris. He made a thorough examination of the bay that he called Astrolabe Bay, set up an observatory on shore, and collected specimens of plants and birds.

One of his most exciting adventures happened when he sailed through French Pass. It took five days to get through the narrow channel where tide rips and currents endangered the vessel. He named the island that is separated from the mainland by French Pass after himself but, as he said, only until the Maori name was known. In later years men insisted on honouring

The *Astrolabe* in French Pass

him by retaining his name, and as D'Urville Island it is known to this day.

The *Astrolabe* sailed through Cook Strait and crossed to the North Island, where D'Urville saw the entrance to Port Nicholson. The harbour had been visited and charted a few months earlier by Captain Herd, who brought a party of settlers to New Zealand. Scared by the warlike Maoris, the settlement they tried to found at Hokianga was soon abandoned.

D'Urville wanted to enter the harbour on the shores of which the capital city was later built, but stormy seas drove his ship onwards. The *Astrolabe* sailed up the east coast, across the Bay of Plenty, along the coast of the Coromandel Peninsula, and into the Waitemata Harbour, where the officers went on shore to explore the countryside. A further excursion was made into the Firth of Thames, and then the ship's prow was turned northwards. D'Urville entered the Bay of Islands and remained there for some time. During his stay in New Zealand he charted many parts of the coast with great accuracy. Thirteen years later, in 1840, he paid another visit to the country and people who had attracted him so much on his earlier voyage.

Maoris visit the *Astrolabe*

Of all the explorers who came to New Zealand, Captain James Cook is the one who is honoured most, not only for his painstaking researches and careful recording of information, but also because of his humanity to the people who lived there, and to his own crew. Next in importance probably comes Captain Dumont D'Urville who showed the same care and humanity to his own men and to the people of New Zealand.

Dumont d'Urville meets the Maoris

## Chapter Four  HOW THE FIRST WHITE PEOPLE SETTLED IN NEW ZEALAND

## The Coming of the Sealers

Sealers at work.

Captain Cook told the people in England how plentiful the seals were in New Zealand and on some of the islands further south. It was not long before sealing ships began to plough the southern seas. In the year 1792 the *Britannia* entered Dusky Sound, where Cook had stayed for some time during his second visit in 1773. The *Britannia* landed a party of men and sailed away to Brazil. About two years later she picked up the lonely shore party and 4,500 seal skins which they had collected during their stay.

Seal skins were worth a great deal of money, ranging from sixteen to sixty dollars each. The owners of the sealing vessels found that it was a profitable business. In a few years there were sealing gangs on both sides of Foveaux Strait, and also on Campbell, Bounty, Auckland and Macquarie Islands.

Seals are mild, inoffensive animals, easily killed, and the slaughter went on year after year without anyone in these southern lands to make laws for their protection. For this reason most of the seals were killed and the trade fell off. By 1820, less than thirty years after the first sealing expedition, they were so scarce and difficult to find that it no longer paid to hunt them.

If we are sorry for the animals that were killed, we must also remember the men who actually hunted them. The captains of the sealing ships often landed them on some rocky, barren island, where they lived in rough, makeshift shelters, barely protected from the storms and bitter winds, until the ship returned for them. For food they had to depend mostly on seal meat, spending their days killing the seals and skinning the carcasses. Sometimes the ship never returned, and unless they were picked up by another vessel, they would die a lonely death of starvation.

Although many of them were rough men, they helped to make New Zealand. Some of them married Maori wives, tamed their savage relations, and helped to stamp out cannibalism. Their descendants are well known in New Zealand.

A sealer and his family.

A lonely sealing gang.

# The Coming of the Whalers

For many years whaling had been carried on in the seas of the Northern Hemisphere. Whale oil was greatly in demand. Towards the close of the eighteenth century a ship bound for Port Jackson (Sydney) ran into a school of whales so large that the sea seemed to be covered with them. The news spread quickly, and soon scores of whaling ships came south to try their luck. By the year 1800 everyone knew that the South Pacific was the best part of the world for whaling.

The whalers soon found that places such as the Bay of Islands in the north, and Akaroa Harbour in the south, were ideal sheltering places for refitting and taking fresh provisions aboard. The Maoris began to know the Pakeha whalers well, but unfortunately their visits did more harm than good, because the Maoris learned some of the worst habits of the white men. The seamen lived a hard life, and for most of them their spell ashore was spent in drinking.

In the year 1827 Jacky Guard, a broad-shouldered, black-bearded sealer was passing through Cook Strait when his schooner was driven towards the southern coast. He expected to be cast on the rocks, but at the last moment the current took him into the calm waters of Tory Channel in the Marlborough Sounds. Guard discovered baleen whales sheltering there, because the cow whales came up the South Island coast every winter to give birth to their calves. He returned quickly to Sydney, laid in a supply of stores and whaling gear, engaged his crew, and established the first shore whaling station in New Zealand at Te Awaiti. Soon these shore

Stripping blubber from a whale.

67

whaling stations were to be found on both sides of Cook Strait and down the eastern and southern coasts of the South Island as far as Preservation Inlet.

Cargoes of whale oil were not collected as quickly from shore stations, but the costs were less, and the life was not so hard. The best of these whalers settled down and married Maori wives. Some of their descendants are amongst the honoured families of our country. The war against the whales came to an end in the 1860s when there were few whales left to be killed. A whaling station at Te Awaiti, equipped with powerful boats, was maintained in the twentieth century, and was closed down only in 1965.

# The Burning of the Boyd

Te Puhi is flogged.

As white men began to make frequent visits to New Zealand, daring Maoris travelled on the big white-winged ships. Some of them even went as far as England and had amazing stories to tell when they returned home. But some of them never saw their own country again. A few of the captains were cruel men who ill-treated their Maori guests and left them in distant countries.

One Maori chief, Te Puhi, had roamed over the world. He sailed back to New Zealand in the *Boyd*. On the way the captain ordered him to be flogged for some fault. He did not realise how much the proud Maori chief resented being punished like a slave.

One day the *Boyd* sailed into Whangaroa in the far north of New Zealand where Te Puhi's tribe lived. The Maoris came round the ship in their canoes and everyone seemed very happy. Some of the sailors went ashore to cut down trees for spars, and with them went a party of Maoris. After travelling through the forest for a while, the sailors sat down to rest, laughing and trying to understand what their Maori companions were saying. Suddenly the Maoris drew their weapons and killed the white men. They dressed themselves in the clothes of the murdered sailors, and hurried back to the shore. Then they rowed out to the *Boyd* and killed nearly everyone on board. Te Puhi's people had avenged his injuries.

That night, as the Maoris danced and sang on the *Boyd*, there was a terrific explosion. Flames leaped to the masthead, and the ship burned and sank. One of the warriors had accidentally set fire to a barrel of gunpowder.

When news of this tragedy was heard by other white men, they were very angry, and sent an expedition to punish Te Puhi's people. Unfortunately the Maori language was difficult to understand, and another village belonging to a chief named Te Pahi was bombarded instead. It is no wonder that after this the Maoris distrusted the Pakehas and that, amongst the traders of Sydney, New Zealand was a place to be avoided.

The Maoris attacking the sailors.

The Maoris on their way to the *Boyd*.

The burning of the *Boyd*.

# The Coming of the Traders

Sealers and whalers were not interested in bartering, except to get food in exchange for clothes, axes, nails, pipes, tobacco and other things that the Maoris had seen and admired. The first real trade in New Zealand came when it was discovered that kauri trees made the best masts and spars – and the British Navy needed masts! You will remember that the sailors of the *Boyd* were on the way to cut down trees for spars when they were killed. It was also found that New Zealand flax made the best rope in the world. The merchants in Sydney began to make plans to get supplies of flax and timber. Since the *Boyd* tragedy traders had been afraid to come to New Zealand.

As time went by a few brave men arrived and set up trading posts, where they exchanged the white man's

*Above:* Cutting down tall kauri trees for ship's masts.

*Left:* Maoris bartering potatoes for a hatchet with a pakeha trader.

70

goods for flax, timber, potatoes, and pigs. A tribe which had its own "Pakeha" was very proud of him, and protected him against the other tribes. But sometimes these traders would break the Maoris' laws, and then they were robbed of all their goods, so it was a dangerous and difficult life for these lonely white men.

What really established trading in New Zealand was the Maoris' love of fighting! Some of the whalers had bought their provisions with muskets and bullets and gunpowder. A tribe which was armed with muskets was able to kill its enemies easily and quickly, and so a great race began amongst the tribes to see who could get the most firearms. It was a matter of life and death for the tribes which had no Pakeha weapons. The Maoris came down from their healthy pas on the hill tops, and lived by the swamps, cutting and scraping flax in a desperate struggle to get enough to buy the precious muskets. The white man now had something that the brown man wanted so badly that the price was increased. Traders often demanded a tonne of scraped flax for a single musket!

Muskets being traded for flax.

Cutting flax for the trader.

# Samuel Marsden, the Maoris' Friend

In the same year that the crew of the *Boyd* were killed at Whangaroa, a Maori chief named Ruatara sailed to Australia from England. When he first arrived in London, he had asked his way to the King's palace, but people laughed at him. He managed to get a passage to Australia on the ship *Ann*, and there he found an old friend, the Rev. Samuel Marsden, Chaplain of New South Wales. Marsden saw that he was looked after, and when they reached Sydney, took him into his home until he was able to arrange for his young Maori friend to be taken back to his home at the Bay of Islands.

Marsden travels by canoe.

Marsden travels overland.

Marsden giving spades to the Maoris.

Samuel Marsden and his friend Ruatara.

Marsden had always liked the Maori men he had seen and befriended. He longed to go over to New Zealand to preach the white man's Gospel to them. When Ruatara left him, he promised to come over soon, but the news of the fate of the *Boyd* reached New South Wales shortly afterwards, and the Governor would not let Marsden undertake such a dangerous trip.

Five years later, in 1814, Marsden made a voyage across the Tasman Sea in a tiny vessel with several missionaries who were to remain in New Zealand. They landed at Whangaroa and there, amongst the very people who had killed the crew of the *Boyd*, Marsden lay down on the shore, wrapped in his coat, and slept peacefully.

On Christmas Day, 1814, Marsden was at the Bay of Islands, and the New Zealanders heard the Gospel story for the first time. Marsden's sermon was translated sentence by sentence by Ruatara.

The great-hearted missionary went fearlessly among the Maoris all over Northland and as far south as Tauranga, travelling by canoe or on foot. Wherever he went he trusted his Maori friends and gave them useful presents such as spades, axes, and nails, and preached the Gospel. During the next twenty-three years Marsden visited New Zealand six times. He encouraged the missionaries who were working, and taught the people himself. Sometimes he was away so long that his friends thought that he had been killed, but he always came back. The Maoris loved him and welcomed him wherever he went. They knew that he was their friend.

The first Christian service in New Zealand.

# The Coming of the Missionaries

It was a dangerous and difficult life for the missionaries. At first they set up their mission station at Paihia in the Bay of Islands. The Church of England missionaries built their houses, taught the Maoris how to plough, sow seeds, and reap the harvest, and at the same time taught them the message of Christianity.

Sometimes their lives were in danger, and often it seemed that they were wasting their time. The tribes

The mission station at Paihia.

Teaching Maoris to cultivate the land.

Learning to read.

Sacking a mission station.

were nearly always at war, and when they got the white man's muskets in their hands, they killed each other much more quickly than in the old days when they fought hand to hand with their own weapons.

In 1823 the famous missionary leader Henry Williams, who had been an officer in the Royal Navy, came to the Bay of Islands. Gradually the work of these brave men began to bring results. The children went to school, grown men and women learned to read and write, and when the New Testament was translated into Maori, many of them could read it in their own language. Some of the Maoris became true Christians. The missionaries were saddened by the battles that seemed to be fought as fiercely as ever between one tribe and another, but sometimes they were able to bring peace. Henry Williams launched a ship which was built at Paihia, and went with the war canoes to stop the battles. A printing press was brought out from England so that parts of the Bible could be printed in the Maori language.

The Rev. Samuel Leigh established the Methodist mission at Whangaroa. The first time he landed he only escaped alive by throwing fish-hooks on the sand and running to his boat while the Maoris stopped to pick them up. A few months later he went back with his brave wife and lived with this fierce tribe. Later the mission station was plundered, and the missionaries, with the wives and children, had to walk across country at night and take refuge with their Anglican friends at Kerikeri. A few years later they began again at Hokianga on the other side of the island. The Roman Catholics, led by a young Frenchman, Bishop Pompallier, came from France in 1838; James Watkin established a Wesleyan mission station at Waikouaiti in the South Island in 1840, and gradually the missionaries went through both islands, taking their message of peace to the tribes.

# The Terror of the North

One of the most powerful chiefs in the northern part of New Zealand was Hongi Hika. He has sometimes been called the Maori Napoleon. Although he never became a Christian, he protected the missionaries. Hongi had made the long voyage to London but, unlike his nephew Ruatara, he had a pleasant trip and he saw the King! He went with a clever man named Thomas Kendall, who was a school teacher as well as a missionary. We have already seen that the Maori language was not easy to understand, and it was even more difficult to write down. Samuel Marsden himself wrote Maori words in a way that we should think very funny, like Duaterra for Ruatara, Shukeehanga for Hokianga, and Kiddeekiddee for Kerikeri. Kendall decided that it was time that spelling was done in a proper way, so he took Hongi and another chief with him to Cambridge in England. With their aid Professor Lee made a grammar of the Maori language.

While he was in London, Hongi had a good time. King George IV showed him through the Royal Armoury, where he saw the muskets and other weapons. Hongi's mouth watered. Perhaps it was then that he first thought how powerful he would be if he owned many muskets. When he left, the King gave the Maori chief a suit of armour and many other valuable gifts. In Sydney, Hongi changed all the presents, except the armour, for 300 muskets.

Shortly after his return to New Zealand he gave the muskets to his warriors, and they set out to try their strength. Their enemies were powerless, and Hongi laid the country waste. The tribes at Auckland and Thames were destroyed, and Hongi's men triumphantly carried fifty canoe loads of their enemies back with them to the Bay of Islands.

On another expedition he travelled to Tauranga. The canoes were paddled up the rivers and dragged overland along the route which is still known as Hongi's Track. The canoes were launched on Lake Rotorua and the Arawa tribe was surprised and defeated. Tribe after tribe fell before Hongi's muskets, and he was the most feared man in New Zealand. In the end Hongi was himself shot, and though he lingered on for months, at last the Terror of the North was dead.

## The Man o' War Without Guns

By 1831 there were many white men in New Zealand. The missionaries taught the Maori people the Gospel of Love. Honest traders bought and sold, and filled ships with produce, timber, and flax to send to Sydney. Unfortunately there were many white men of a different kind. Some were convicts who had escaped from New South Wales. Others were deserters from the whaling ships. These men brought nothing but harm to the Maoris. And all the time other countries were looking enviously at New Zealand, thinking what an important and valuable colony it would make.

In 1833 James Busby was sent over from New South Wales. He was called the British Resident, and it was his job to maintain law and order among the white men, and to protect the Maoris from cruel and unscrupulous adventurers. Missionaries and honest white men also needed protection from people of their own race, and from the warlike Maoris.

Poor Busby had a very hard time. He had no policemen and no soldiers to help him, but he did his best. He was given very little help by the Governor of New South Wales, and he found it almost impossible to carry out the tasks for which he had been sent. Over and over again he asked for people to be sent across to New Zealand to help him, but in vain. He has been nicknamed "a man o' war without guns".

One of his ideas was to try to unite all the northern tribes. He called the chiefs together and got them to sign what he called a Declaration of Independence. The Governor of New South Wales laughed at it, and called it a "paper pellet", for a reason we shall see in the next section—but it was still a good idea.

Busby's own house was broken into and robbed, but by the end of the eighteen-thirties the better white settlers, backed by the missionaries, decided that if there were no police, they would become policemen themselves, and try to see that dangerous convicts and the rougher sailors were kept in order.

## The Man Who Wanted To Be King

When Missionary Kendall was at Cambridge, a young Frenchman, the Baron de Thierry, gave him $2,000 to be spent on trade goods, and asked him to buy some land for him in New Zealand. Two years later the Baron received a letter from Kendall saying that he had not been able to buy as much land as he had hoped, but that for thirty-six axes he had secured 16,000 hectares. Nobody seems to know what became of the rest of the money!

De Thierry explains his plans.

Busby meets Darwin and FitzRoy.

The road at Hokianga.

In 1834 the Baron arrived in Sydney and wrote to James Busby telling him he was about to sail for New Zealand in an armed vessel, to set himself up as Sovereign Chief of the country. Busby was alarmed by this letter. It was at this time that he persuaded the chiefs to sign the Declaration of Independence.

Week after week passed by. Busby waited anxiously for de Thierry's armed vessel to arrive. At last, in December 1835, a man o' war sailed into the Bay of Islands. But it was a British vessel, not a French one. It was commanded by Captain Robert FitzRoy, and on board was Charles Darwin, who afterwards became a famous British scientist. He had his Christmas dinner with the missionaries at their inland settlement at Waimate.

Another two years passed by before the Baron arrived. He landed with about ninety followers at Hokianga on the west coast, opposite the Bay of Islands. De Thierry was full of promises – open ports, free trade, and no taxes. Unfortunately for him and fortunately for Mr Busby, no one took him seriously. He began to build a road to the Bay of Islands, but his money was spent long before the road was finished. The Maoris would not let him have his 16,000 hectares because they said his old second-hand axes were only a kind of deposit on the purchase.

In the end they took pity on the poor, deluded Sovereign Chief and gave him a few hundred acres as a consolation. In later years he went to Auckland and became a music teacher.

You may not think that this is an important part of our history, but it is, for it made the British Parliament feel that it would not like to see the French flag flying over the country that Captain Cook had claimed for King George III.

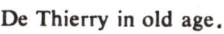

De Thierry in old age.

# The Coming of a Governor

On 29 January 1840, Her Majesty's Ship *Herald* sailed into the Bay of Islands. On the deck stood Captain William Hobson, hero of many naval battles. He had been sent to this little-known country as Governor. The British people had at last agreed with Mr Busby that something more must be done to protect Englishmen and Maoris alike. They realised, too, that if they sat still and did nothing, New Zealand might be claimed by some other country.

A number of boats put off from the shore, and Captain Hobson was greeted by Busby, the missionaries, Mr Clendon, the American Consul (so many American whalers visited the Bay that they had their own Consul), and other important people. There were other white men, however, who resented the coming of a Governor. There were "land sharks" who robbed the Maoris of their land, and quarrelsome ones who feared the British Law that Hobson had brought with him.

The man who stood on the deck of the *Herald* was Captain Hobson, but when, the next day, he landed at Waitangi, he became his Excellency the Governor. He arranged at once for a great meeting of all the chiefs in the district for the following Wednesday, when he would explain to them how Queen Victoria (Kuini Wikitoria the Maoris called her) would protect them and their lovely country from bad men.

H.M.S. *Herald*.

80

On the next page we shall see what happened on the most important Wednesday in the history of New Zealand. While we wait for the great meeting, let us look at our first Governor. He determined to do his best for both Maori and Pakeha and the Queen he served. He governed the new colony for only a little time, for he became ill, and in 1842 he died at the age of fifty-nine.

The best thing that was ever said about this honest man was in a letter which the chiefs of Auckland sent to Queen Victoria when he died, asking for another Governor to be sent to them:

"Let him be a good man. Look out for a good man – a man of judgement. Let not a boy come here, or one puffed up. Let him be a good man, as this Governor who has just died."

# The Treaty of Waitangi

On that famous Wednesday, 5 February 1840, the lawn in front of the British Residency was bright with colour. Sailors from H.M.S. *Herald* had put up a large tent, and naval officers with gold braid and cocked hats, soldiers with red coats, Maoris with brightly-coloured blankets, and missionaries and settlers dressed in black and white, stood waiting for the arrival of the Governor.

Governor Hobson came out of the Residency with Captain Nias of the *Herald*, James Busby, the Rev. Henry Williams, and Bishop Pompallier. Everyone crowded into the tent. The Governor stood up and read the Treaty while Henry Williams translated it into Maori. It said that Queen Victoria wished to protect the Maoris and their property, and asked them to live peacefully with her white subjects. She asked the Maoris to accept her as their Queen and in return she would see that their lands were protected; if they wished to sell, the land would first be offered to the Queen at a fair price so that everyone would be satisfied; and that the Maoris would have the same rights, and the same protection as her white subjects.

When Governor Hobson had finished, a number of chiefs stood up, one after the other, and said that if they signed this Treaty, white men would take away their lands and make them slaves. It looked as though all the Governor's work was in vain. Then a young chief stood up. His name was Hone Heke. He said that unless they chose the Queen for their friend, their country would be taken from them by some other nation, which would not care for their rights. Another chief, wise old Tamati Waka Nene, urged the people to accept the Treaty. He turned to the Governor and said, "I say to you, sit, remain, be to us a father, a judge, a peacemaker."

Other chiefs followed, some for the Treaty and some against. On the following day there was more speech making, and at last the Treaty was agreed to by over forty leading chiefs. Some who had been taught by the missionaries were able to sign their names; others drew the pattern of their tattoo marks.

The man who prepared the Treaty was James Busby. His work was over, for the man o' war without guns had been followed by a man o' war with guns. While we gratefully remember our first Governor, let us never forget the man who prepared the way for him.

Hone Heke, the first chief to sign the Treaty.

# Brown and White Men
## Living Together

There were many important chiefs in other parts of New Zealand besides the forty who had signed the Treaty. Governor Hobson had been told that the country was not to be taken away from the Maoris by force, but with their own consent and goodwill. Of course a few chiefs could not sign the Treaty for all the Maoris in the country. Hobson sent some of his most trusted officers with it to every part of the country. First they went to places where missionaries lived, so that the Treaty could be fully explained. It was at Kaitaia in the far north that the chief Nopera told his people, in the beautiful Maori way of speaking, that "the shadow of the land goes to the Queen, but the substance remains with us". Further and further south Captain Nias of H.M.S. *Herald* and Major Bunbury took the Treaty, until they reached Stewart Island, by which time it had been signed by over 500 important chiefs.

The Treaty of Waitangi has been called the Magna Carta of the Maori people. In New Zealand strong tribes had conquered the weaker ones; strong countries often won and held new lands by conquest; yet here was Britain promising a small, brave, but mostly unarmed people that they could remain in peaceful possession of their lands. In order to protect them from dishonest buyers, the Pakeha Government promised to buy the land at a fair price, and to sell it again to the settlers. Some land was not allowed to be sold, but was to remain the property of the Maori people then living, and of their descendants for ever.

In later years there was trouble over the land, and the Maoris fought against the Pakehas, so that the Queen's soldiers were brought to New Zealand to protect the settlers. But that was not the fault of the Treaty.

## Chapter Five HOW THE FIRST PLANNED SETTLEMENTS WERE FORMED

### *Disappointed Settlers*

In the year 1826 a small group of about fifty colonists had come to New Zealand to find some place to make a home for themselves. They arrived in the tiny ship *Rosanna*, under the command of Captain Herd, calling first at Stewart Island, and sailing up the east coast, until they reached the Hauraki Gulf.

The shores of the Waitemata Harbour would have provided good fertile land, but as soon as they went ashore they saw the bleached bones of Hongi's victims lying thick around the ovens, and they hurried northward again to the Bay of Islands. There they met the missionaries, but still there was no welcome for them. The missionaries feared that white people would show a bad example to the Maoris who were just beginning to follow the teachings of Christ.

So on they went, these lonely saddened people of the *Rosanna*. They rounded North Cape and sailed down the west coast until they came to the Hokianga Harbour. Then came news that the Wesleyan missionaries at Whangaroa had been driven away from the mission station. What a country it was for settlers! They talked about it among themselves and decided that New Zealand was no place for honest, hard-working colonists.

Captain Herd and most of his settlers sailed out of the harbour and left New Zealand far behind them. Today all that we have to remind us of that tiny settlement of long ago is a point of land in Hokianga Harbour called Herd's Point.

Captain William Hobson, the first Governor of New Zealand, who founded a capital in the Bay of Islands, and transferred it soon afterwards to Auckland.

# The Founding of a Capital

After the signing of the Treaty of Waitangi New Zealand became a British colony, and required a capital. Governor Hobson chose Okiato, a tiny settlement near the trading station of Kororareka, as his first capital and renamed it Russell after the British Colonial Secretary Lord John Russell.

It was soon realised that this was not the best place for a capital, and having heard that there were good sheltered harbours further south on the east coast of the North Island, Hobson set sail with some of his officers on a voyage of discovery. The shores of the Waitemata Harbour seemed to be the best place, and the Maoris who lived there were anxious for the Governor to come and live with them.

The Governor favoured a locality somewhere near the head of the long harbour, but Felton Mathew, the first Surveyor-General, wanted him to choose Panmure. Suddenly all their plans were upset. Hobson was taken seriously ill, and the Government ship had to sail back to Russell.

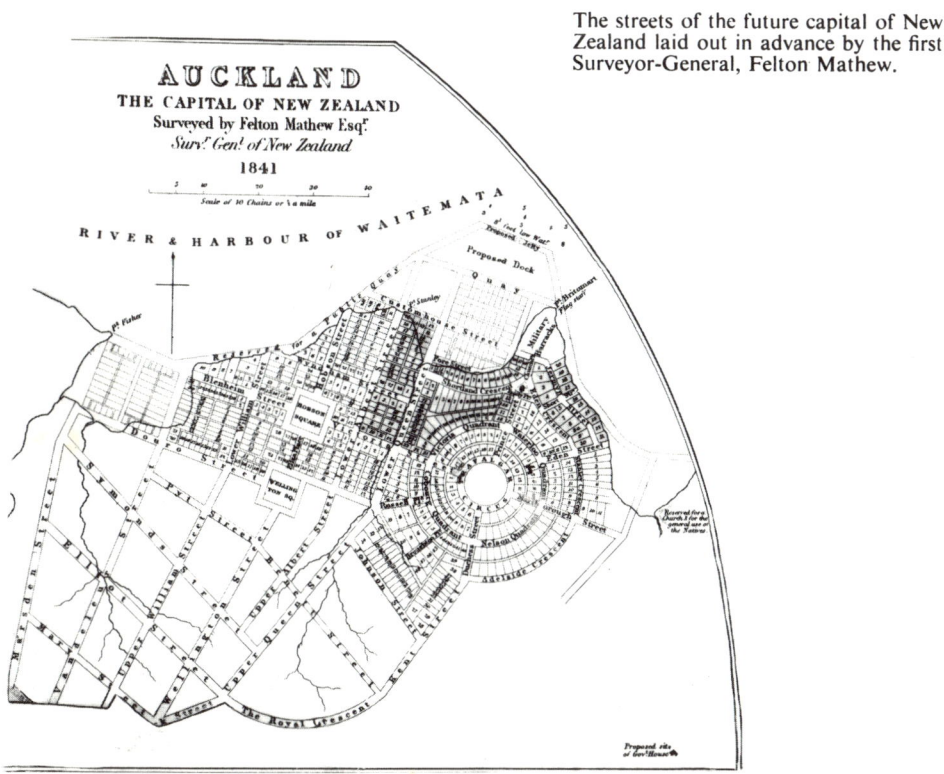

The streets of the future capital of New Zealand laid out in advance by the first Surveyor-General, Felton Mathew.

After a while Felton Mathew and other officials were sent down to look at the harbours of Whangarei, Mahurangi, and Waitemata. The Surveyor-General came back and reported that, in his opinion, some place on the Waitemata would be best. By this time the Governor was recovering from his illness, and in July 1840 he sailed south to establish his capital where the city of Auckland now stands.

Two months later the barque *Anna Watson* left Russell with seven Government officials, thirty-two workmen and their wives and families. The ship anchored off Point Britomart, which was removed some years later to make more room for the growing city. On 18 September a flagstaff was erected on the point, the land was bought from the Maori owners, the flag was hoisted, cheers were given, and Her Majesty's health was drunk. In the afternoon there were canoe and boat races on the harbour, and everyone was in holiday mood.

But what a tiny little village it was – just a few tents half hidden in the fern, close to the stream which flowed down the valley where Auckland's main shopping street now runs. In Mechanics' Bay the workmen, or mechanics as they were called, built their houses, but the

The infant city of Auckland begins to spread over the hills and gullies. When the "officials" and "mechanics" first settled here, there were only a few tents and raupo huts among the fern. In this painting we can see that later settlers have arrived, because there are ships in the harbour, and many well-built homes. St. Paul's Church stands in a prominent position on Point Britomart.

Felton Mathew built his home in Emily Place on Point Britomart. Later it was sold to Colonel Wynyard, who is seen in this picture with his family. The drive to the house is guarded by sentries. The tower of St. Paul's is in the background.

Government officials kept to themselves in Official Bay.

Felton Mathew set to work to plan the streets of the capital of New Zealand; the workmen built the Government store at the foot of Queen Street, erected houses for the officials, and put together a house, which had been brought out from England in parts, for the residence of the Governor.

Auckland was founded in a different way from all the other settlements, as we shall see later. The first comers were not really settlers at all, but Government officers and workmen.

# Auckland

## The Coming of Settlers

Sir John Logan Campbell, the "father of Auckland".

It was not long before settlers came flocking to Auckland. The fact that it had been chosen as the capital attracted all kinds of people who realised that, if they could buy land cheaply, its value would soon grow. Some were known as "land sharks", whose only object was to make money as quickly as they could. Others were a fine type of settler. One of these was John Logan Campbell who, with his partner William Brown, had begun to farm the island of Motukorea (later known as Browns Island) before the capital was founded. Brown and Campbell were amongst the most prominent citizens in Auckland. When Sir John Logan Campbell died in 1912 at the age of 94, he was known as the Father of Auckland.

The first Government land sale was held a few months after the flag had been flown on Point Britomart, and city sections fetched high prices which supplied the Government with plenty of funds.

It was in 1842, two years after its real foundation, that two ship-loads of settlers arrived from Scotland. They came on the ships *Jane Gifford* and *Duchess of Argyle* and for many years these immigrants were known as "Duchesses" and "Lady Giffords".

These Scottish settlers had a hard time during this early period. There was little work and less money, and the streets were hardly more than lanes and ditches. The new arrivals were employed turning muddy tracks into roads. Married men received 2s. 6d. (25c) a day, but single men only 1s. 6d. (15c). There were many single young women amongst the 535 Scottish immigrants, but they did not

90

The emigrant ships *Jane Gifford* and *Duchess of Argyle* arriving in Auckland harbour in 1842 (from a painting by Captain M. T. Clayton in the Colonists' Museum, Auckland).

The Albert Barracks, a stern reminder to the early settlers that they might at any time have to defend their homes against the Maoris. But in Auckland town the Maoris were friendly. A number of them are watching the soldiers on parade at the barracks.

remain unmarried for long. The settlers who had already arrived were mostly young men, and soon many weddings were being celebrated in St Paul's Church on Point Britomart.

Business houses began to flourish. At Official Bay beautiful homes had been built by the waterside. Felton Mathew's house cost £2,000 ($4,000). It had French windows opening on to a wide verandah, and a lawn dotted with flower beds and young trees and planted with vines. At Government House there were dances and balls, where women could wear their prettiest dresses.

At Mechanics Bay canoes with potatoes, fruit, fish, and firewood were paddled ashore, and light-hearted Maoris laughed and sang as they traded with their Pakeha friends.

But on the ridge above the town there was a fortress, manned by soldiers. There were rumours of war in the north, where Hone Heke had cut down the flagstaff at Kororareka as a protest against the white man's rule.

# Trouble Between Maori and Pakeha

Shortly after Captain Hobson died, a new Governor, Sir George Grey, was appointed. He was very much respected, for he was fond of the Maori people and did a great deal to help them. At the same time he was fair to the white people.

Sir George Grey soon found that he had many problems to face. The powerful Maori tribes in the Bay of Islands were very disappointed when the capital was removed to Auckland. Few ships came to the bay, and the chiefs found that they could not earn as much money as they had in the past.

One of the chiefs, a nephew of the famous Hongi Hika, whose name was Hone Heke, thought he would teach the Governor a lesson. Heke had been the first to sign the Treaty of Waitangi, but he was so disappointed at what had happened afterwards that he gathered his young men together and climbed the hill at Russell where the Government flagpole was standing. He cut it down to show the white men that there were Maoris who would not obey them. The flagpole was put up again, and again Heke cut it down.

The Governor sent soldiers to protect it, but Heke cut down the flagpole for the third time. This was a sign of war. The Maoris and the red-coat soldiers fought each other, and a number of people were killed at Russell. Bishop Selwyn, who had just been appointed Bishop of New Zealand, came to help the wounded. For several months there was fighting between Maori and Pakeha, until at last peace was declared.

Then there was trouble further south, on the island of Kapiti, where a fierce Maori chief, Te Rauparaha, lived. He had become the terror of the Maori tribes from Wellington to far down in the South Island. Te Rauparaha has been called the Maori Napoleon, for he was a skilled warrior and conquered several other tribes.

On one of his expeditions to the South Island Te Rauparaha overcame the tribes who lived near the Wairau Plain, and claimed their land by right of conquest. The white settlers in Nelson knew nothing of this. They had found there was not enough land for farming near Nelson, and thought that the land they had purchased included the Wairau Plain. They sent several of their people to survey it.

When Rangihaeata, a nephew of Te Rauparaha, heard that the land was being surveyed, he hurried to the Wairau. Both Maori and Pakeha believed they had a claim to the land. A rifle was accidentally fired, and a battle began. About twenty of the white men were killed.

These were uneasy days for the settlers. At one time the people of Wellington feared that Te Rauparaha and Rangihaeata would raid their town. Fortunately many of the Maoris were friendly, and Octavius Hadfield, a missionary at Waikanae, persuaded Te Rauparaha to change his mind.

The kind of home that many of our great-grandparents first lived in.

# The First Wakefield Settlement

In the southern part of the North Island settlements of another kind grew up quickly. Wellington, Wanganui, New Plymouth, as well as Nelson in the South Island, were all Wakefield Settlements. Christchurch and Dunedin grew up in the same way but were not formed by the New Zealand Company.

There was a big difference between these places and Auckland, which at first was populated mainly with Government officials. To understand how the Wakefield settlements were born we must go back to England, to see what was being done by a man named Edward Gibbon Wakefield.

As a young man Wakefield had lived a careless life, but as he grew older he became thoughtful and observant. He saw that there was a great deal of poverty and ill health in England, and he realised that there were too many people in the country. Men could not find work, or had to accept jobs which were so badly paid that they could not support their families. There was a great deal of misery in the poorer parts of the big cities of England and Scotland at that time.

"If only I could find a way for good hard-working men to go overseas it would be a grand life for them," he thought, "and there would be more room and work for those who remained behind."

A cartoon in *Punch* showing the poverty of people in England in the middle of the nineteenth century. There was another part of the cartoon which depicted the "ideal" life in the colonies—a life that was made possible by the vision and energy of Edward Gibbon Wakefield whose portrait appears on the right. (Engraving by B. Hall, Rex Nan Kivell Collection. Australian National Library, Canberra.)

Wakefield had many important friends, and he talked to them and began to interest them in forming a New Zealand Company.

"How would it work?" they asked.

Wakefield explained. "We must find money to pay the passages of the right kind of people to New Zealand. If only they could have such a chance they would make good. But there are few who can pay the cost of sailing half way round the world. There will have to be money, too, to buy land from the Maoris."

"And how will we get it back?" they asked.

"When the land goes into production, these immigrants will soon have enough to feed their own families, and will be able to sell the rest of their crops. In this way they will get money to pay us back. We must plan everything carefully before we choose them. The land will soon increase in value, but in fairness to the Maoris some land must always be kept for them. The main thing is in the planning, so that our immigrants know what to do as soon as they arrive there."

This seemed such a good idea that interested people joined together to form "The New Zealand Company". E. G. Wakefield's brother, Colonel Wakefield, went out in the *Tory* to buy land near Cook Strait ready for the first settlement. He called at Queen Charlotte Sound and then crossed to Port Nicholson, a sheltered harbour at the southern end of the North Island. He was welcomed by the Maoris, who were persuaded to sell all the land in sight for less than £400 ($800) worth of trade goods – clothing, fish hooks, tobacco, muskets, even red night-caps and jews harps.

A typical early settler's house with thatched roof. Husband and wife are carving a home for themselves in the bush in the most primitive conditions.

# Wellington

The New Zealand Company's survey ship *Tory* in Queen Charlotte Sound before her arrival in Port Nicholson, where the capital city of Wellington now stands. After a painting by Charles Heaphy.

The *Tory* was soon followed by the *Cuba*, which brought men to survey the land and decide where the sections were to be laid out. Then came the first ship load of settlers, then another and another – nine of them altogether – bringing hundreds of men, women, and children to this new land of promise.

After the long and uncomfortable sea journey, how glad they were to be on land once more! They erected tents, and camped on the beach at Petone, calling their little settlement Britannia. It was a real camp. They lived in tents, cooked in the open air, and caught eels, fish, and birds for food as a welcome change from the ship's provisions. Soon the tents had to give way to huts. The Maoris were glad to make rough shelters of manuka and tree ferns in exchange for a blanket. It was hard work for mothers and fathers; and for children too, but the youngsters revelled in the life in the bush and on the sandy beach.

When the bush sections were chosen, Father felt that he was a real pioneer as he felled the forest trees, made a tiny clearing and sowed his first crop. He had to work hard, for his money – which he spent on food – did not last long. At least it was better than starving in England while looking for work. But if the children felt that it was like a picnic, they found that all picnics must come to an end. The southerly gales blew in from the harbour entrance and the Hutt River flooded their homes. The men decided that Petone was not the best place, and after much thought it was decided that the settlement would have to be removed to the other side of the harbour, on the flat land below the hills, where the Maoris had built their pas at Pipitea and Te Aro. The settlers shifted their tiny village, and the town of Wellington, named after England's great soldier, was founded.

The Hutt Road taken at the gorge looking towards Wellington, about 1843. A steel engraving by H. Melville, after an original by S. C. Brees.

Houses were built, roads were formed, and shops erected along "The Beach" – where Lambton Quay curves through the city of today.

With 1,000 people living in Wellington it was soon found that laws had to be made and officers appointed to see that they were kept, and to decide the disputes that sometimes arose. As we know, New Zealand was now a colony of Great Britain. Governor Hobson was alarmed when he heard that the New Zealand Compan·'        s were making their own laws. There could be only one C New Zealand. He sent soldiers under the command c loughby Shortland to see what was happening, and to m the settlers realised that the Government had authority of New Zealand.

Unfortunately Shortland did not get on very well · Wellington. They felt that Russell was a long way they made their own laws to see that order was trouble with the Maoris and trouble among th Shortland's criticisms; but they were loyal have liked Governor Hobson to have live' felt that such a fine, growing township islands was really the place for the car needed help, for after the signing

Governor had proclaimed that the Maoris could sell land only to the Government. Wakefield had bought the Company land direct, and the settlers were not sure whether they would be allowed to remain in possession.

It was in these difficult times that the people courageously set about the building of their homes, farms, and businesses, little knowing that the city they were founding would eventually become the capital of New Zealand.

Thorndon Flat and part of Wellington in April 1841. The original water-colour by Charles Heaphy was painted on Clay Point, now the corner of Willis Street and Lambton Quay. Harbour reclamations now extend far to the right, but the curving line of Lambton Quay still preserves the original shape of "the Beach" as shown in this picture.

# Wanganui

# and

# New Plymouth

Edward Jerningham Wakefield.

The New Zealand Company founded another settlement in the North Island, at the mouth of the Wanganui River. At first Colonel Wakefield thought that he had bought all the land as far north as Kawhia; but he soon found that there were many tribes who had their own rights to much of this land.

Wakefield's son, Jerningham, was sent north to Wanganui, where he made arrangements to buy land near the river mouth. Two months later, in May 1840, he made another trip from Wellington, this time in a schooner laden with £700 ($1,400) worth of trade goods. The supplies were taken ashore in canoes and divided into heaps by the principal chief, so that there would be a fair share of goods for each tribe or sub-tribe. In this simple manner Wakefield paid for land for a settlement at Wanganui.

The Maoris were wildly excited by these wonderful gifts from the Pakeha. They danced round the heaps, and every now and again someone would snatch a mirror, a handful of nails, or a pipe. The principal chief, Kuru, saw that his people might get out of hand before the distribution was made, so he warned Wakefield and his friends to go back to the schooner.

Kuru was right. Excitement mounted to fever heat, and the chiefs could not keep order.

"Seven hundred naked savages were twisted and entangled in the mass like a swarm of bees," Jerningham Wakefield wrote. "Weapons were brandished, goods smashed, blankets torn, and sometimes a frenzied man was seen to leap over the others, or perhaps thrown over their heads, on to the heaps of goods."

The next day all the goods had gone – and so had the land. Kuru and his people must have realised that for the sake of a few trinkets they had given away their age-old heritage. He thought hard about it, and no doubt consulted with his people, for the following day he brought thirty pigs and ten tonnes of potatoes and gave them to Jerningham Wakefield, saying that it was "gift for gift".

"No. The land has been sold," Jerningham told him; "you have put your mark on the papers, and the land belongs to the Company. It will be a good thing when the Pakehas come to live with you. It will bring you mana and much wealth. As for the pigs and potatoes, we will buy them from you for our people in Wellington."

And so the town of Wanganui was born. At first it was called Petre after a director of the New Zealand Company. Towards the end of 1840 a number of families made their homes there, after tramping along the beaches from Wellington.

The Company's method of buying land was not really satisfactory. The Maoris felt that they had not been treated fairly, and in later years much trouble came to the white settlers as a result.

Twenty years after its establishment Wanganui is still a primitive settlement, but the river mouth has become a busy port. Stacks of timber can be seen by the water's edge waiting to be taken away by ship. The photograph shows the present site of the Moutoa Gardens and Ridgway Street.

In England a number of people from Devon and Cornwall asked the New Zealand Company to buy land for them in New Zealand. In 1840 an exploring party set out from Wellington and spent a whole month travelling up the west coast. They explored the land around Cape Egmont and chose a place on the coast not far from the mountain. There they brought 20,000 hectares of land for goods worth £500 ($1,000). To this place, which was called New Plymouth, in March 1841 came the men and women of Devon and Cornwall.

Missionaries landing on the Taranaki coast. From an oil painting by George Baxter 1844.

## The French at Akaroa

In the early 1840s many thoughtful people were worried at the condition of England's poorer folk. They began to make plans for buying land in distant colonies, to which workmen could migrate with their families.

England was not the only country that was making such plans. It was from France that some of the first permanent settlers came to New Zealand.

In the year 1838, two years before the signing of the Treaty of Waitangi, a French captain called at Akaroa, the deep, sheltered harbour on Banks Peninsula. Captain L'Anglois saw what a fine harbour it would make, and how its fertile land and bush-covered hills would make an ideal home for a colony of French settlers. Before he left he bought the Peninsula from its Maori owners for £240 ($480) worth of trade goods. When he arrived back in France he sold this land to a Company, and shortly afterwards the settlers

101

sailed for New Zealand in the cruiser *Comte de Paris*, accompanied by another warship, *L'Aube*, commanded by Captain Lavaud. They had visions of the whole of the South Island being proclaimed a French possession.

In the meantime British statesmen had been busy. While the French ships were still on the high seas, the Treaty of Waitangi, by which New Zealand became a British possession, had been signed. When Captain Lavaud arrived at the Bay of Islands in advance of the *Comte de Paris* – which was making direct for Akaroa – he learned that the Maoris had signed the Treaty. He thought that if he acted quickly he might still claim Banks Peninsula as a French possession.

As soon as he heard of the intentions of the Frenchmen, Captain Hobson sent the British warship H.M.S. *Britomart*, under Captain Stanley, to Akaroa.

The *Britomart* had crowded on her sails, but lost canvas and spars in a gale, and was swiftly overhauled by *L'Aube*. Then Lavaud was becalmed. When he sailed up Akaroa Harbour he found that the *Britomart* had already arrived, and the Union Jack was floating on a mast on Green Point.

When the settlers arrived on the *Comte de Paris* shortly afterwards, they found that their dreams were not to come true. Banks Peninsula was part of the British possession of New Zealand.

It must have been a great disappointment to them, but this story has a happy ending. The French were permitted to settle at Akaroa on British soil; and here they made a home for themselves and were kept in touch with their homeland by the visits of French whalers.

Akaroa from Cemetery Hill 1853. From a watercolour by William Leigh.

# Cherry Farm

We can easily imagine the difference between the small groups of huts of men on the shore whaling stations and the large, well-ordered settlements.

Before the Treaty of Waitangi, there was one little settlement in the South Island that was halfway between these two extremes. In the days of the rough sealing gangs, young Johnny Jones saw a good deal of the southern waters of New Zealand. He was ambitious and hard working, and after some years as a waterman, carrying passengers across Sydney harbour, he became a whaler.

Three years later, in 1838, he made good use of his money and his talents. On the east coast of Otago, at the little port of Waikouaiti, there was a whaling station that had not paid its owners very well. They were in financial difficulties, and Jones was able to buy the station cheaply. But it was not as a whaling station only that he used this land. He realised, as few people had done up to that time, that some day New Zealand would be an important farming country, and that already good money could be made by supplying ships with farm produce. He bought a large block of land from the Maoris and became a land owner on a big scale.

Back in Sydney he interested people in his farm in Otago, and early in 1840 his brig *Magnet* brought a band of settlers to his farm at Waikouaiti. They came prepared for hard times, but perhaps few of them realised how hard their work would be. There were no houses to go to; as soon as they arrived the settlers had to build wattle and daub huts, driving posts into the ground and tying sticks across them. The spaces were filled with clay or mud mixed with grass.

The ground was broken up with adzes and hoes and sown with grain. When the corn came up the children of the settlers had to drive off the flocks of parrakeets that settled on the fields.

Though they grew much of the food they needed, the settlers depended on visiting ships to bring many of the necessities of life. When no vessels came, they went hungry.

There was no school for the children and no building to use as a church, until Jones helped the Rev. James Watkin to establish the first southern mission station.

Waikouaiti in 1873. From a painting by John Kinder.

A short distance away were the shore whalers, but the farmers saw little of them at Cherry Farm, the name Jones gave to the tiny settlement in memory of one of his whaling captains, who had been killed by the Maoris in Cook Strait.

There they lived – a tiny, isolated community almost at world's end, cultivating the land and rearing cattle and sheep. Though it was a small settlement it was an important one, because a few years later, when the Presbyterian Free Church Settlement was established in Otago, much of the produce for it came from Cherry Farm.

John Jones

# Nelson

Life was hard in the settlements. Usually a tent was the only place in which to live until the first rough whares had been built as some shelter from rain and wind. Water had to be fetched from the nearest stream, and cooking was done in a "camp oven" – a round iron pot placed in the ashes of the fire. The whole family would often live and sleep in a single room and long hours had to be spent in clearing the bush and trying to plant crops.

But for most of the settlers the difference from their old life in England was wonderful. Instead of unending work in factories and the dirt and smoke of slums where children had no place to play, there were green forests and golden beaches, and the song of the

The arrival of the *Whitby, Will Watch* and *Arrow* in November 1841. From a watercolour by Charles Heaphy.

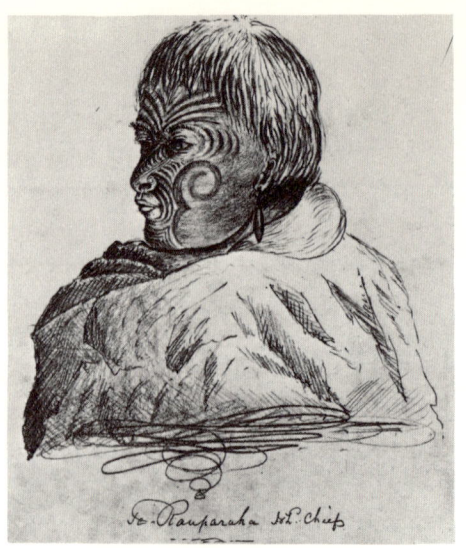

Captain Arthur Wakefield

Te Rauparaha. From a pencil sketch by Charles Heaphy, owned by W. F. Airey.

birds in the clear air of morning. No wonder that mothers and fathers in England longed to bring their families to such a lovely, spacious land. No wonder that young men and women felt that parting from their families and the long months at sea were worth while, because of the opportunities they hoped to find in this new country half way round the world. In later years news of troubles with the Maori people had spread to England; but at this stage thousands of adventurous English men and women applied to the Company for the chance to emigrate to New Zealand. It was at this time that the New Zealand Company was formed to buy land and send settlers to New Zealand. The Company sent Captain Arthur Wakefield, a brother of the man who had founded the Company, with a party of surveyors to choose a site for a settlement.

They decided on a place in the South Island in Blind Bay. Captain Wakefield visited Kapiti Island, and got Te Rauparaha's permission to survey the land. This great fighting chief of Kapiti had made raids into the South Island, and was regarded as the principal chief of much of the land south of Cook Strait. Captain Wakefield lost no time in surveying the land, and in 1842 the first four emigrant ships arrived inside the Boulder Bank which protects the harbour of Port Nelson.

The town sites were quickly decided on, and soon the plain at the foot of the hills was dotted with primitive houses. The town was called Nelson after England's great naval hero, just as Wellington had been named after her greatest soldier.

Nelson in the 1850s from the Port Hills. (Tyree Collection.)

When the settlers arrived at the makeshift little town, no houses awaited them, and they had to wait many months before food could be obtained from their gardens, and years before they could make a living from their country sections. While they waited, their savings were spent, and for many families there were times when they were hungry, with no money to buy goods, and no work to be had anywhere.

But gradually the land was cleared, the crops harvested, the homes improved, and the settlement began to flourish and spread north-westward. It spread eastward, too, as far as the Wairau Valley. There the surveyors met opposition from the Maori owners, and because tempers were roused, and someone fired a musket by accident or in panic, twenty Pakehas were killed by the Maoris, who believed that their land was being stolen from them.

# Edinburgh of the South

A year after the Wairau affair one of the Company's surveyors, Frederick Tuckett, left Nelson on a scouting expedition far to the south to choose a site for a Scottish settlement. After looking in at Port Lyttelton he continued his voyage. Leaving his ship, the *Deborah*, at Waikouaiti, he struggled through the bush until at last he was able to look down on Otago Harbour and the bush-covered slopes of the Peninsula beyond. Soon afterwards he set out on a journey further south, spending the first night in the rain among the scrub on what is now Dunedin's busiest corner. He went overland, across the Taieri Plain, down the Taieri Gorge, and on by ship as far south as Ruapuke Island near Stewart Island. After many adventures he came back to Otago Harbour, satisfied that this was the best place for a southern settlement.

Tuckett bargained with the Maoris for the sale of land, and later Colonel Wakefield came down and paid them for it. As a result of his experiences in the North Island he realised how important it was to make sure that the Maoris knew what they were selling. Mr Symonds, who had been present at the founding of Auckland, and two other officials went with him to see that everything was done properly. They went over the land carefully with the Maoris, deciding on the boundaries and explaining what was being done. Taiaroa, one of the leading chiefs of Otago, at first wanted a million pounds ($2,000,000) for the land! Finally the chiefs settled for £2,400 ($4,800), which was a very fair price – no muskets or red cotton night-caps, but a good price in cash, with everyone happy and contented. Most of these chiefs were Christians, and great credit was due to the Rev. James Watkin, the Methodist missionary, for the peaceful sale of the land.

Before the first settlers came there were a number of white people in these parts – a missionary, whalers, and pioneers like the Andersons of Andersons Bay, who had made a lonely home for themselves at the head of Otago Harbour. A little further north Johnny Jones had established his whaling station and his own little settlement at Waikouaiti.

The hardy independent Scottish settlers who founded Otago had rebelled against State control of their Church, and wished to make a home for themselves where they could work and worship as they pleased. Four hundred ministers gave up their churches and their homes in order to form the Free Church of Scotland. Amongst them was the Rev. Thomas Burns, who had a large church and manse and a comfortable living. He went to live in a tiny house and held his services in the open air, where he and his people could be free to serve God as they thought best. These were the type of men and women who composed the members of the Otago settlement.

There were many obstacles to be overcome before all the arrangements were completed, but at last, in 1848, the first emigrant ships left the old country for New Zealand.

"What shall we call our settlement?" they had asked. "We are going to found a Scottish town on the other side of the world. Let us call it New Edinburgh."

But William Chambers, a famous Scottish publisher, had a better idea. "Call it Dunedin," he said. "That is the old Gaelic name for Edinburgh."

The arrival of the *Philip Laing* at Port Chalmers on 15 April 1848. The *John Wickliffe* is already at anchor.

# Dunedin

Dunedin was a settlement with a difference. The land was bought wisely and well, for the organisers had learnt from the mistakes of earlier emigrants. Revenue from the sale of the land was used not only to pay the costs of the expedition but also for churches, schools, and roads. Because of the high aims of its founders Dunedin is noted for its fine churches and its advanced educational system. In later years the first University in New Zealand was established in Dunedin.

The first two emigrant vessels left Britain in November 1847. The *John Wickliffe* arrived at Port Chalmers in March 1848 from England, and the *Philip Laing* three weeks later from Scotland. The pioneer men and women soon made a typical Scottish community, hard-working, thrifty, generous, and devoted to their Church.

They set to work as soon as they landed, and in a few months their homes were dotted about the shores of the upper harbour. Some of the small huts were made of tree-fern trunks cut in two lengthways, placed side by side, with the crevices plastered with mud. The more substantial ones were built of wattle and daub.

Rev. Thomas Burns

Dunedin from Little Paisley about 1849. A lithograph after an original watercolour by E. I. Abbot.

The settlers were more fortunate than those in townships in the North Island. There was no trouble with dissatisfied Maoris, and no escaped convicts from New South Wales. Things did not always go smoothly, but into their carefully ordered community had come some of the finest people of Scotland, headed by far-sighted leaders.

As in all the other settlements there were many difficulties to overcome. At first there were no streets, and the site of the settlement was covered with bush and scrub. When the country sections were opened up, years of back-breaking toil were required to bring the land into cultivation. It was some time before bullock carts could be used to take produce and goods in and out of the settlement.

One of the early settlers who lived about thirty kilometres from Dunedin worked early and late on his farm. Every Sunday he walked to church in Dunedin. He cut his wheat with a reaping hook, made a flail for threshing from two sticks joined by means of the skin of an eel, and ground his grain on a hand mill. When he made butter for the first time, he carried a 32 kilogram keg five kilometres to the nearest calling place for ships.

111

It was hard work that made the earliest settlers so healthy and prosperous. Three years after the founding of Dunedin gold was found at Goodwood, and five years later at Mataura. At that time the world was in the grip of gold fever, from the Golden Gate in California to the rich fields of Australia. The good Presbyterians of Dunedin were not excited. At first most of them preferred their quiet, hard-working lives to the risk of a rush of lawless men in their settlement. By 1861, however, rich finds had been made in Central Otago, and the call to wealth could no longer be resisted. The fever spread and men of all kinds joined in the rush to the goldfields, or worked to supply the diggers with food and other goods. The Province became wealthy because of these discoveries.

It was mostly through the hard work and simple living of her people that the city prospered. Dunedin became such a wealthy community that in later years it was able to find money for many of the enterprises of northern towns. In the city itself many fine houses and buildings were erected. They are still standing as a monument to the industry of the first citizens of Dunedin.

Dunedin's main thoroughfare, Princes Street, in 1861.

# The Canterbury Pilgrims

Christchurch was the last of the "Four Cities" to be founded. The settlers who came to the province of Canterbury were humorously known as the Canterbury Pilgrims, but they were not the first families to make their home in this part of the country.

As early as 1843 there were a few homesteads on Banks Peninsula, and one lonely house on the Canterbury Plains. This house belonged to two brothers, John and William Deans. Their pioneer home is still to be seen in the populous suburb of Riccarton in Christchurch.

Even before this time, as we have already seen, there was a French colony at Akaroa.

The real founders of the city of the plains were the Canterbury Pilgrims. To learn why they came to New Zealand we must go back to England again. A group of influential men formed what was known as the Canterbury Association. The New Zealand Company had already bought a large area of land on the Canterbury Plains from the Maoris for the sum of £2,000 ($4,000). Through the Canterbury Association this land was sold to the colonists. So many settlements had been formed by this time that the New Zealand Company

The first houses on the Canterbury Plain. The house with the chimney was built at Riccarton by the Deans family in 1843. A sketch by E. M. Hocken after the original by J. Gridland.

Immigrants coming ashore at Lyttelton from the *Cressy*. The barracks can be seen in the middle distance. An etching by Thomas Allan from a water-colour by William Fox.

had learned many good lessons. They had made plenty of mistakes, but what was most important, they were ready to profit by them. For this reason the Canterbury settlement, like the one at Otago, was well planned, right from the beginning. The money which was received from the sale of sections was divided into six parts. One-sixth paid for the cost of surveying and making roads, two-sixths was spent on bringing labourers and servants who would make useful helpers for the colonists who had money of their own, another two-sixths was spent on churches, schools, teachers, and ministers. The last sixth was kept by the Company.

John Deans

114

No settlement is ever better than its leaders, and the Canterbury Pilgrims were fortunate in having chosen John Robert Godley for this position. He spent only two years in Christchurch, but during that time he led them wisely. The first two years were the hardest, and none worked harder than Godley. At the end of that time he was able to leave them, knowing that they could look after themselves. His statue in Cathedral Square shows how much they loved and admired him.

Christchurch was planned as a Church of England settlement, and the stately Cathedral in the heart of the city shows how everything centred round the Church. The Archbishop of Canterbury was the patron of the society, Sumner was named after his home, and the principal streets bear the names of Church of England Dioceses in various parts of the world.

It was also planned as a typically English settlement, and there is no place in New Zealand which looks more like an English city. The River Avon flows peacefully through the flat plain which was once an enormous swamp, bordered by English willows and beautiful gardens. Everywhere one sees the stately stone buildings which remind us of an old-fashioned English town.

John Robert Godley

# Christchurch

We might easily think that the flat well-watered plain, the freedom from disputes from the Maoris, and the careful planning of the Colony would make things easy for the Pilgrims. It is quite true that they were spared some of the hardships of the earlier settlers, for over 100 men were at work for a year before the arrival of the Pilgrims, surveying land, making roads, and putting up barracks to accommodate the first arrivals.

But let us look at the men, women, and children who arrived in the first ships. They disembarked at Lyttelton and went to the barracks which had been made ready for them. They could not stay long, because they had to make way for those who came on the next ship, so the hillsides were soon dotted with white tents, whares, and sod huts.

A view of Christchurch from a settler's balcony in 1852, sketched by Dr A. C. Barker.

During the fine weather it was one long picnic, especially for the children, but when a south-west gale came, tents disappeared and homeless people sought shelter in the huts of their friends.

At first it was intended that the settlement should be formed at Lyttelton, but soon it was seen that it was only on the plain that there would be room for the shiploads of immigrants. There was no tunnel through the hills. Heavy goods were sent by sea to Sumner and up the River Avon, but the colonists themselves struggled up the Bridle Track which climbed steeply up the hills.

When they arrived at the "city", they were scarcely any better off. Tall flax, toetoe, and tussocks covered the part now known as Cathedral Square. One early arrival walked right through the heart of the "city" asking people the way to Christchurch. But gradually cottages like the letter V turned upside down began to be dotted over the plain.

There was plenty of water, but no drainage, and the people's health began to suffer, until a plumber drove gas pipes into the ground and discovered limitless supplies of pure artesian water forty feet below the ground.

Then came an "invasion" from Australia. Australian colonists were having a hard time and many of them began to cross over to Canterbury, having heard of the fertile plains of the South Island. This was against the rules of the Canterbury Association, which had intended Christchurch to be a Church of England settlement, but Godley saw that such immigration could not be stopped. He boldly altered the rules so that they could come freely amongst his own people. Later, when gold was discovered in Australia, many of the Shagroons, as they were called, and some of the Pilgrims crossed the Tasman to try their luck on the goldfields.

As the years rolled on, the Pilgrims made more roads and bridges, drained the swamps and built houses, schools, and churches. They cultivated their land and drove their herds of cattle and flocks of sheep further and further towards the distant hills. And as they worked, Christchurch gradually grew into a beautiful city with lovely parks and stately buildings, to become a little bit of old England in New Zealand.

# Danish and Scandinavian Settlements

By 1870 the struggling little settlements of the 1840s had become prosperous towns and cities, and New Zealand had become a well-governed, well-established colony, with good communications throughout the country and overseas. We might think that the pioneering days were over. Great tracts of land had been brought under cultivation, and most of the difficulties faced by the first settlers were over. There had been Maori wars, but these were happily ended. There had been a financial depression, but gold discoveries had been made, and the people of New Zealand faced the future confidently.

Most confident of all was the Prime Minister, Julius Vogel. "Borrow and Spend" was his motto. Vogel dreamed that New Zealand would become a great nation. The country was still covered with bush and swamp in many places, and even some of the most important towns were isolated from their neighbours. Vogel borrowed money to build roads and railways that would open up the country and increase its prosperity.

Vogel discovered that it was easier to get money than men, so he began another policy – that of immigration. British immigrants were encouraged to come to New Zealand. Half their fare to New Zealand was paid by the Government and young women were given a free passage. And still there were not enough workmen for roads and railways!

In 1866 the Superintendent of the Province of Wellington (in those days each Province had its own Council or Parliament) invited a party of Danes to come to New Zealand to live. Five years later 120 Danes settled in the Manawatu district, and another party went to Mauriceville in the Wairarapa. These people were real pioneers. Few of them could speak English, but they came prepared to make homes for themselves. We should remember them with admiration, for they came to a foreign land, met incredible hardships, and overcame them.

At Mauriceville the hardy people from Denmark worked in the heavy bush and made homes for their families there. During the week they earned money by building a road northwards through the dense forest. As the road got further away from their settlement, they had further to walk, until they found that they had to leave in the early hours of Monday morning and return home late on Saturday. On Sunday they worked all day clearing their sections. The women and boys and girls had a long way to walk over muddy tracks and through rivers to sell farm produce when at last they were able to keep cows on their cleared land.

In 1872 more Danish, Norwegian, and Swedish settlers came to Hawke's Bay and were sent to little clearings in the Seventy Mile Bush which later became known as Dannevirke and Norsewood. The men went first, and felled the huge forest trees. The timber was cut into lengths and split into long slabs, and was used to build their tiny two-roomed homes.

We can scarcely imagine the hardships that were faced by the pioneers – the unending toil, the never-ending mud in their forest home. They had brought some of the customs and traditions of their Fatherland to New Zealand, but they also became true New Zealanders. The descendants of the 4,000 Danes and Scandinavians who came to our country between 1872 and 1882 have now been scattered to every part of New Zealand, taking with them the spirit of their forefathers.

A scene in the Forty Mile Bush near Mauriceville in the Wairarapa in the 1870s. This was the site of a Scandinavian settlement. In place of the dense forests busy townships have grown up on the fertile, grassy plain.

119

## Chapter Six

# HOW NEW ZEALAND BECAME A NATION

## *The Country Begins to Grow Up*

As more and more settlers came to New Zealand from England and Australia, there were busy scenes in the towns. Land was bought and sold, ships were built, and men began to sell the products of their country farms.

Many of the things that could not be made here had to be brought from overseas, while products of the land were sent away from New Zealand to pay for what was imported. Ships were needed for coastal and overseas trade; roads had to be built for wheeled traffic; mails had to be delivered, which meant that post office and telegraph lines were required; and policemen were needed to keep order.

These public services cost money, which meant that taxes had to be collected to pay for them, and laws were needed to decide how money was to be raised and how it was to be spent. In other words, a Parliament was needed. Because there were few roads, it took a long time to travel from one part of the country to another, and one central parliament was not enough.

## *Provincial Councils*

In addition to the central Parliament, each of the six provinces—Auckland, Wellington, New Plymouth (later called Taranaki), Nelson, Canterbury, and Otago—had its own Provincial Council. It may seem strange that a young country with such a small population needed six Provincial Councils as well as a Parliament or House of Representatives in Auckland. This was because it took so long for people to travel by coastal boats and coaches from one part of the country to another that one central Government was not able to do everything that was needed.

Government House, Auckland, about the year 1842.

Parliament Buildings, Wellington, continue to expand. This architectural drawing shows the new additions of the 1970s, with the older portion on the right.

Parliament made laws to control the buying and selling of Crown (Government-owned) lands, collected taxes and customs duties, provided a Department of Justice, a postal service, and controlled weights and measures. Even when the capital, where Parliament met, was shifted from Auckland to a more central position in Wellington, in 1865, it was still necessary for the provinces to control their own affairs.

Each province elected a Superintendent and a Provincial Council of at least nine members. In later years four more provinces, Southland, Westland, Marlborough, and Hawkes Bay were formed. Southland had difficulty in paying its way, and was glad to join Otago again. The period of the Provincial Councils lasted from 1854 until 1876. For more than twenty years, therefore, New Zealand had a "federal" system of government, in which the provinces governed their own local affairs but joined together to send their representatives to the central Parliament, which made laws for the whole country.

It was too clumsy and wasteful a system for a small country, of course, and as communications improved and population increased, the provincial governments were abolished.

## Central Government

When the Provincial Councils came to an end, the power to make all laws passed into the hands of the House of Representatives, but there were still some controls over it. There was another "House", called the Legislative Council. Its members were not elected, but were appointed by the Governor and the House of Representatives. Each new law (known as an Act) that was passed by the House of Representatives had to be approved by the Legislative Council and signed by the Governor before it became one of the laws of the land. At first the collection of laws, or constitution, of Great Britain also formed the constitution of New Zealand, but new laws were gradually introduced to suit the needs of a young, quickly-developing country.

Since New Zealand became a self-governing colony there has only been one important change in the system. This happened in 1950 when the Legislative Council was abolished, leaving the House of Representatives as the only law-making body in the country.

An engraving from the *Illustrated London News*, showing a "bivouac of surveyors".

# Exploration

The white people in New Zealand wanted to know as much as they could about their new country. In the beginning they had to depend upon the Maoris to help them. The Maoris had made tracks through the dense forest, and had crossed wide rivers in canoes or by swimming. The first white explorers followed the Maori trails, and made long journeys to unknown places, discovering new land where farms could be made.

Some of the earliest journeys were made by missionaries as they visited the different tribes. We have already seen that Samuel Marsden travelled long distances in the northern part of the country on his visits to New Zealand. Another missionary, who was also a naturalist and a famous explorer, was William Colenso. He made lengthy journeys in Hawke's Bay, through the bush and over the ranges, where travelling is difficult even today.

George Augustus Selwyn, the Bishop of New Zealand, was another great traveller. On one occasion he travelled from Wellington to Auckland by canoe and on foot, as also did James Buller, a Wesleyan missionary.

Then there were geologists and explorers, like Ernst Dieffenbach, who was employed by the New Zealand Company. He was the first man to climb Mount Egmont, and later he explored the country round Lake Taupo and Rotorua.

In the South Island Thomas Brunner and Charles Heaphy spent years in the dense forests, living off the land and discovering a great deal about the West Coast.

The South Island was very different from the North Island. As there were high mountain ranges to cross, explorers and surveyors were employed by the Provincial Governments to find passes across the Southern Alps.

The explorers were followed by surveyors, who drew maps and planned routes for roads and railways. One of the surveyors was Arthur Dudley Dobson, who discovered Arthur's Pass, which leads from Canterbury to Westland. Dr Julius von Haast was the first to cross the pass that was named after him.

We owe a great deal to these explorers, who endured hardships and risked their lives in the service of their country.

# *Gold*

New Zealand was slowly growing into a land for farmers. Life in the country was difficult, because there were so few roads. It takes a long time to turn forest land into prosperous farms. New Zealand was so far away from all other countries except Australia that it was costly to export farm produce.

Then something happened which made New Zealand much richer, and brought many men from other countries. Gold was found, not just in one place but in several parts of the country. Thousands of men gave up their work and went out with pick and shovel and a few provisions to try to find the gold that would make them rich. As soon as the news reached Australia, every ship brought eager gold-diggers to New Zealand.

Gabriel Read

A miner's tin dish and cradle.

A religious service at Gabriel's Gully, 14 July 1861. From a painting by W. Wilson in the Museum of the Otago Early Settlers' Association, Dunedin.

They had to travel long distances, carrying all their tools and provisions, through bleak difficult country, sometimes crossing mountain ranges and dense forests. Some were fortunate, but the diggers were often bitterly disappointed because they did not "strike it lucky". Then they went away and tried their luck somewhere else, as new discoveries were made.

Gold was found in Central Otago by a prospector named Gabriel Read. Instead of keeping his discovery to himself, and making himself rich, he wanted to share it with others. He went back to Dunedin and told people about his find, bringing samples of the gold with him.

Almost overnight Dunedin was emptied of men, as they rushed to the rich new field that was called Gabriel's Gully after the discoverer. The gold-miners went further and further inland. Others grew rich by carting provisions over the rough country to sell to the gold-miners.

Further finds of gold were made in the Nelson Province and on the west coast of South Island. Millions of ounces were dug from the ground and washed from river sand. Canvas towns were built, banks were set up, gold was bought, and armed escorts were provided to protect the gold convoys on their way to the cities.

The gold was exported, and a great deal of money began to come to New Zealand. For a few years the gold fever raged in New Zealand. Then gold became more and more difficult to find as the richer fields were worked out, and men went back to their ordinary work. Some had become wealthy, but others were a great deal sadder and wiser. Ever since those far-off days some gold has been won each year. It has played an important part in the history of New Zealand.

Bell Block Stockade, New Plymouth, in 1860. Painting by W. Diamond.

# Fire in the Fern

Most of the goldfields were in the South Island, which began to prosper. Times were not so good in the North Island. Children of the early settlers were growing up and starting out for themselves, and more immigrants were coming from overseas. The towns were busy, and there was need for more land for farming. The Maoris realised that their land was very precious to them. They had sold a great deal of it, but the money had all been spent and their land was gone for ever!

The Maoris had been cheated by some white men, and they tried to get possession of the land again. Even when the Maoris had not been cheated, it was difficult for farmers to buy new land from them. This meant enmity between white and brown people. If there was a war, it would spread like "fire in the fern". The settlers armed themselves, and women and children were taken into armed forts or stockades for safety.

There was a lot of fighting in Taranaki. The Maoris were very clever at bush warfare, while British soldiers, with their red tunics and their own way of fighting, had a difficult time. The settlers who took up arms, and were called the Armed Constabulary, were much more successful.

At last the war in Taranaki was over, but more troubles arose in the north. A number of tribes chose a Maori King, because they wanted to rule over their own land. The King movement began in the

126

Waikato, and soon there was fierce fighting going on in this part of the Auckland province.

Many soldiers had come from Great Britain, but the Maoris fought bravely against them. Then a Polish officer, Major von Tempsky, and a settler, Captain Jackson, formed a unit called the Forest Rangers. These New Zealanders became as skilled in bush fighting as the Maoris. Finally the Maoris were defeated at the battle of Orakau, and some of their land was taken away from them.

At this time a Maori prophet called his people to battle. He said that if they cried "Hau hau!" and did what he said, they would be protected by the Angel Gabriel from the white men's bullets. It is for this reason that these Maori warriors were called Hauhaus. Only one more fight ever took place between Maori and Pakeha, when the notorious warrior Te Kooti terrorised the East Coast districts for several years without being caught. So peace at last came to the country.

The fighting had all taken place in the North Island. Many of the South Island settlers felt it was unfair that they should have to pay some of the heavy costs of a war which was fought only in the North Island. But gradually all New Zealanders realised that they were one country and had to share their responsibilities. As the bitterness of the war died away, Maori and Pakeha learned to work together and to respect each other.

The Forest Rangers engage a Maori war-party. From an original painting in the Auckland War Memorial Museum.

# Public Works

For many years fighting had taken place in the North Island between Maori and Pakeha. It died down, and then flared up again. Then at last the wars were over, but unfortunately, peace did not bring plenty.

A slump, or depression, a time when work is hard to get, often follows a war. In the 1880s New Zealand had a depression. Men could not find work, their families were often hungry, and farms had to be abandoned. One cause of the trouble was the high cost of sending New Zealand produce to be sold on the other side of the world.

When bad times come a leader is usually found, even though it may take a long time before he is able to bring prosperity back to his country. On this occasion the leader was a newspaper editor named Julius Vogel. He became Prime Minister and put into practice a number of new ideas that were badly needed at this time.

When everyone was feeling miserable, and saving every penny, Vogel borrowed millions of dollars; he brought thousands of immigrants to New Zealand and began to build roads and railways all over the country. Many people shook their heads and thought he was being foolish, but things began to prosper, and money flowed freely once more. We are still benefiting from Vogel's public works.

Later there was another severe depression. And then something really important happened . . . . refrigeration.

Men at work in a cutting on the North Island Main Trunk railway line.

"Refrigeration" is a long word, but we must remember it, for it is one of the most important things that ever happened to New Zealand.

During all the years that the white people had been living in this country, they had grown wheat and other crops and had farmed sheep and cattle. They had been able to ship and sell their farm products, grain and tallow and hides and wool and cheese, to England and other countries overseas. But they were not able to ship butter and meat, because no one knew how to keep these two products fresh while on the long sea voyage through the tropics.

Then clever men invented machinery which froze or chilled meat and butter, keeping it fresh for weeks or months on end. Imagine what this meant to the farmers! Now they could send meat and butter as far as England or America, knowing it would be fresh when it arrived. It meant that there was a new market for a different kind of product that would bring a great deal of money into New Zealand.

The first shipment of frozen meat was sent from Port Chalmers in 1882. Nowadays New Zealand exports more than five hundred thousand tonnes of meat and two hundred and fifty thousand tonnes of butter in refrigerated cargo ships each year.

Early refrigerating machinery.

129

# The Maori People

As we have seen, peace had been made between Maori and Pakeha. They had fought against each other, not always understanding each other's problems. The settlers had been hungry for land that was going to waste and which, with hard work, they could turn into profitable farmlands, on which the prosperity of New Zealand depended. They did not see why it should be kept in forest just for the sake of a few Maoris.

But to the Maoris it was their heritage, the Forest of Tane, which provided them with food and shelter and was their home. The fierce wars between Maori and Pakeha in Taranaki and Waikato had arisen because of quarrels over land. The Pakehas had won the wars; but the land south of Waikato, which we still know as the King Country, because so many of the Maori King's followers lived there, was reserved for the Maoris, and for many years no Pakeha dared set foot there.

Gradually the old quarrels were forgotten, and Maori and the Pakeha learned to respect each other. Many of the Maoris learned the white man's ways, and yet were still proud of their own Maori way of life.

One of the greatest of them, whose name was Timi Kara (James Carroll), became a member of Parliament, and served his people's interests there. For his services, not only to the Maoris but to all the people of New Zealand, he was knighted by the Queen, and became Sir James Carroll. He was the first of a number of Maoris who have served their own people well. Others were knighted in later years for the work they did for their country.

# The End of a Century

On the West Coast of the South Island, mining towns still flourished. The miners were self-reliant, blunt and honest, and warm-hearted. Of all the West Coasters the most loved was Richard John Seddon— an outspoken, fearless champion of poor and unfortunate people. He was ready to spend his life helping them. He stood for Parliament, was elected, and eventually became Prime Minister.

Success didn't change Dick Seddon. He had many ideas for helping poor people. Soon after he became Prime Minister he introduced pensions for widows and old people, and a law called the Factory

Act, which put an end to the bad conditions under which many people had had to work. The popular, stout-hearted West Coaster was affectionately nicknamed "King Dick".

Hard times came again for a while, and people were frightened that they might lose their money. It was rumoured that the Bank of New Zealand had hardly any money left and people rushed to draw out their savings. This made matters much worse. Unless something was done quickly, it was certain that many people would lose their savings. A special session of Parliament was held, and an Act was passed allowing the Government to lend money to the Bank. This saved the day, and the Government became part-owner of the Bank of New Zealand.

While Seddon was Prime Minister war broke out between Great Britain and the Boers in South Africa and fierce fighting took place. South Africa was a long way off but New Zealanders were proud to be part of the British Empire. Immediately war was declared, there were many volunteers, and a contingent of men soon set sail and fought side by side with the British soldiers.

A country is just like a human being. It has to start as a baby, depending on help from the motherland. As the years go by, it grows up and becomes able to look after itself. This is what happened to New Zealand. After sixty years it had indeed grown up. By the year 1900, exciting things were beginning to happen.

The first contingent of volunteers in the South African War leaving Karori, Wellington, in October 1899.

# Beginning Another Century

One of the first events of the twentieth century was not important in itself but because of what it stood for. The Duke and Duchess of Cornwall and York, who later became King George V and Queen Mary, visited this country. New Zealanders discovered that, though they were proud of their own progress, they had a great loyalty to England. They felt they were indeed a part of the British Empire. There was mourning throughout the land when Queen Victoria died in the same year.

People were beginning to think of others too, and there were wise statesmen who framed laws to bring justice and help to those who were in want. The Old Age Pensions Act had been passed, so that elderly people who could not work were given money to live on. New Zealand had showed in several ways it was able to lead the world. Free, secular, and compulsory education for all her children, both Maori and Pakeha, had come as early as 1877. Some years later, every British subject who was over twenty-one years of age was entitled to vote at elections.

One of New Zealand's greatest men living at this time was Dr Truby King. He spent most of his life working for babies, teaching mothers how to feed and care for them. With the help of the Governor's wife, Lady Plunket, the Plunket Society was formed, and specially trained nurses gave advice and help to mothers. Before he died Sir Truby King had the satisfaction of knowing that there were fewer deaths and less sickness amongst babies in New Zealand than in any other country in the world.

Perhaps the best sign that New Zealand had grown up came in 1907, when the Motherland made her a Dominion. This meant that New Zealand became quite self-governing. She could make her own decisions on everything, but the old loyalties remained. New Zealanders were proud of being British subjects, and honoured the royal family. The Governor-General represented the reigning King or the Queen. New Zealand took some responsibility for her own defence. Though she still depended on the Royal Navy to guard the seas, she was ready to send soldiers to the aid of the Motherland in time of need.

# The First World War

One day a farmer was working on top of a haystack, when a telegram came for him. As he was busy, one of the farm labourers put it on his hay fork, and handed it up to him.

When he opened it, he found it was an invitation to stand for Parliament. William Ferguson Massey, for that was his name, accepted the invitation and was elected. He was an honest, hard-working man, and when the party he represented came to power, he became Prime Minister from 1912 to 1925.

His greatest test came when England declared war on Germany in August 1914. Although New Zealand was farthest away of all the British Dominions, she was the first to join Britain in the struggle.

Within a few days of the declaration of war a small force of New Zealand soldiers sailed for Western Samoa, which was a German dependency. New Zealand soldiers took possession of the territory in the name of the British Empire—and until a few years ago had the responsibility of governing Samoa. Now Western Samoa has grown up too, and governs itself, though New Zealand still helps it in many ways.

The war, which lasted from 1914 to 1918, is known as the First World War, because so many nations were drawn into it. When Germany invaded Belgium and France, British forces went to France to oppose the German army.

New Zealand soldiers served in many countries, but principally in France, where the war was waged for four years in cold, muddy trenches. In contrast to this, battles were fought in Palestine under the hot sun. The Maoris fought side by side with their Pakeha friends, and everywhere the soldiers from "Down Under" were known as brave fighters.

The action in which New Zealand distinguished themselves most was at the siege of the heights of Gallipoli, against the Turks, who were on the side of Germany. The New Zealanders fought alongside Australians. Ever since, Australian and New Zealand soldiers have been known as ANZACS (which stands for Australian and New Zealand Army Corps). The action was not successful because the Turks had taken up positions that could not be overcome. Great heroism was shown by the Anzacs when they were forced to retreat.

During the retreat Lieutenant Freyberg, a young New Zealand

soldier serving with the British forces, swam several kilometres at night to light flares on some lonely beaches, so that the Turks would think that the allied troops were landing there. For this deed Bernard Freyberg was awarded the D.S.O. Later he gained the V.C. and in the Second World War he commanded the Second New Zealand Division in North Africa. Still later, in 1946, Lord Freyberg was appointed Governor-General of New Zealand.

The historic landing of the Anzacs at Gallipoli. From the painting by Cyrus Cuneo.

## Between Two World Wars

It was a happy day for people in the allied countries when the war ended in 1918. The war with Germany had been won. No longer would wives and parents dread the arrival of a telegraph boy who might be bringing a telegram to say that one of their loved ones was wounded, or missing, or killed in action.

But there was still another trial that New Zealand, as well as many other countries, had to face. A world-wide influenza epidemic, which was so severe and so widespread that it was known as a pandemic (the word "pan" meaning "everywhere") swept through New Zealand. Schools and churches, picture theatres and public halls were closed, people were forbidden to gather in crowds, but still the epidemic grew. There was hardly a household in the country where there was not at least one sick person. Hospitals were overcrowded, and doctors and volunteer workers toiled night and day. By the time the epidemic was over, seven thousand people had died.

When the first world war was over, and the soldiers had come back to their homes to begin work once more, New Zealanders began to make up for the time that had been lost. During the war no roads or railways had been constructed, few houses had been built, and there was a great deal to do, even in repairing the machines and factories that had been neglected.

Although war is a terrible thing, science makes great advances at such a time. Far-sighted people were already making plans to put the many discoveries of the past few years to work so that the country would benefit by them. Doctors had discovered how to cure many diseases; aeroplanes were beginning to prove a reliable method of transport; new ways of making roads and railways and bridges had been developed. Motor transport had already begun to take the place of horse-drawn traffic. Men who had learned the discoveries of modern science had come back to their own country, eager to use their skill in the service of New Zealand.

With all the discoveries of science to help them, such men began to change the habits of their countrymen. It was difficult for some of the returned soldiers, of course. They had become unsettled after four years of war, and were unwilling to go back to office desks. The Government helped many of them to buy farms; but there were so many who wanted to be farmers that the price of land rose to such a high level that they were unable to make the farms pay. Some of the returned soldiers lost all their money and suffered a great deal of hardship. But in time New Zealand settled down to living at peace.

Many things that we now take for granted first began to be made in the 1920s and 1930s. At first there were no refrigerators in homes, very few motor cars, no motor highways, no radios, no television sets, no aeroplanes. New Zealand was preparing for the days when science and industry would work together to change the life of every man, woman, and child in the land.

The widespread use of electricity was probably the most important thing that happened. New Zealand is one of the fortunate countries of the world because it has inexhaustible, swift-flowing rivers that can be harnessed to produce electricity.

Streets and homes were lit by this new source of light. Trams and some railway lines were electrified, and machinery and factories began to be driven by electric power. Ranges, radiators, vacuum-cleaners, and later radios, refrigerators, and many other electric domestic appliances came into use. Farmers in many parts of the country were able to milk their cows, and light and heat their homes by means of electric power.

A New Zealand town about the year 1920.

# A World-Wide Depression

At the end of the 1920s New Zealand shared a very unpleasant experience with many other countries. There was another depression. Many people found it impossible to get work. Fortunately New Zealanders were not as badly off as the people of some countries, but it was a difficult time. There were families who had very little food. The Government gave employment for a few days in each week to those who were out of work, and work-camps for unemployed men were set up in different parts of New Zealand.

When hard times come, people hope that the Government will be able to put things right again. Slowly the country began to regain its prosperity, and then came a change of Government. For many years the Labour Party, which mainly represented the working people, had only a few members in Parliament. In 1935, when an election was held, the voters decided that it was time the Labour Party had a chance to see what it could do. The Labour candidates were elected with a big majority of seats in the House of Parliament.

Under the leadership of Michael Joseph Savage, and later of Peter Fraser, the new Government began to make many changes. Government Departments ran services that had previously been conducted by business houses. Imports were controlled, to make sure that the country did not overspend its income, and Social Security was introduced. This was tremendously important to New Zealand.

You will remember that many years before, Richard Seddon had started a system of pensions for elderly people who had no money of their own. The Labour Government decided that everyone must give part of his income to the State. Then, when people were sick or getting old and couldn't earn anything, the country would give them money that they had collected from them and from others when they were young and strong. In this way richer people helped those who were not so well off. New Zealand then became known as the "Welfare State". Once again she had led other countries in showing how she could look after sick and elderly people.

## Chapter Seven  THE PAST AND THE PRESENT

## Transport by Road

In the nineteenth century New Zealand was still a young country. Roads were expensive and there was little money to spend on them; but until they were made it was not possible for productive farm lands to be developed. In some places toll gates were erected, and people who travelled on the road were charged for using it. One of the first toll gates was built in 1863 at Kaiwharawhara, on the Hutt Road, between Wellington and Lower Hutt. A two-wheeled vehicle drawn by a horse was charged a shilling (10c) every time it used the road; a four-wheeled cart with two horses two shillings (20c), which was a great deal of money in those days. No one liked paying tolls, and when the Hutt County Council built two more toll houses, the indignant people of Wellington and Lower Hutt threw the gates into the harbour.

The road through Otira Gorge, 1875. From the painting by Thomas Cane.

Other ways of paying the costs of road-making had to be found. When the Provincial Councils were abolished the central Parliament was able to finance the work by taxation, which spread the cost evenly over the whole country. This was important, because road-making was much more expensive in some provinces than in others, because of mountain ranges, swamps, and dense bush.

By the beginning of the twentieth century most parts of New Zealand could be reached by road. Some of the arterial highways were metalled but country roads were often formed of clay, and in winter were almost impassible to everything except bullock teams.

Then the motor car made its appearance on the scene, and the

rapidly increasing use of cars and trucks speeded up road construction. The first car to travel from Wellington to Auckland took more than eight days to make a journey of 800 kilometres. Today a fast car covers the distance in a few hours, but the journey has been shortened by many kilometres. The highway sweeps smoothly like a ribbon throughout the length of the land.

In 1922 a Main Highways Board was set up. The users of the roads had to pay for their construction, upkeep, and improvements by means of a tax on petrol. Every year the need for good roads becomes more important to the prosperity of our land.

Cobb & Co's coach on the summit of the Hope Saddle.

Motor coaches at the time of the First World War.

Typical scenes on New Zealand roads and highways.

# Transport by Rail

By the 1860s, when there were good roads in some parts of New-Zealand, one could travel fifty kilometres by coach in a single day, and people began to feel that they were living in an age of speed! Many settlers had never made a train journey, even in England, because there were few railway lines there in the 1840s. New Zealand-born children had never seen a railway engine.

News of the growth of railway traffic in Britain was eagerly read, and men began to dream of what New Zealand would be like if the iron horses could fly over the shining rails at 100 kilometres an hour. But the land was mountainous and heavily forested, and it was unbelievably difficult to construct a permanent way for trains. Unlike the roads, which could go up and down and wind round sharp bends, the railway tracks had to be carefully graded and gradually curved. This meant that hills had to be removed, bridges built over ravines, and long tunnels bored through the mountains.

When men make up their minds that they really want something, nothing will stop them. In 1863 a short railway line was built from Christchurch to Ferrymead, a port on the Heathcote River. The little engine *Pilgrim*, named after the "Pilgrims" who came to Canterbury, drew goods trucks and tiny passenger carriages between the town and the port. Four years later a tunnel two and a half kilometres long had been bored through the Port Hills, and the railway line to the port of Lyttelton was open for traffic. It is difficult for us to realise what an incredible task this had been for a small new-born settlement.

A wood engraving in the *Illustrated London News*, showing the "vast crowds" that came to see the opening of the Christchurch–Ferrymead line in 1863.

*Above:* A four-engined train noisily puffing its way up the Rimutaka Incline on a one in fifteen grade in 1939. Today swift diesel-electric engines race through a nine kilometre tunnel from the Wairarapa to the Hutt Valley and the capital city.
*Below:* The age of steam has almost vanished. Clean and powerful diesels have now replaced the romantic steam engines of the past.

In those days New Zealand was divided into several provinces, each with its own government. None of them had much money, but they were all anxious to develop their natural resources. Unfortunately more than one gauge (that is, the width between the rails) was used, and before long it was evident that the central government would need to insist on a standard gauge being used throughout the country.

One of New Zealand's most brilliant politicians, Julius Vogel, worked hard to abolish the separate governments so that roads and railways could be built without provincial jealousies. He drew up a Public Works policy, borrowed money from England, and arranged for thousands of men to be brought out to New Zealand to build a railway system throughout the land.

Many people thought that Vogel would make the country bankrupt. Ten years later 2,000 kilometres of track had been laid, and a large part of New Zealand was being served by this modern form of transport. Once again the surveyors risked their lives in rugged country, this time planning a route for the iron horses.

In the years that followed, some world-famous engineering feats were accomplished – the Raurimu Spiral, which enabled trains to climb 250 metres in a distance of five kilometres; the Rimutaka Incline, where "Fell" engines climbed up into the mountains, and vans with brakes that clung to a central rail kept the trains from racing down out of control; 80 kilometres of tunnels including the Otira Tunnel, eight and a quarter kilometres in length, which pierces the Southern Alps, and the later eight and a half kilometre tunnel which replaced the steep grades on the Rimutakas; and nearly 3,000 bridges, some of which are spidery viaducts that carry passengers and goods trains over steep chasms.

Today there are 90,000 kilometres of roads and 5,300 kilometres of railway track, but the steel rails carry more goods traffic than all the roads put together.

A six-car multiple unit electric train brings workers to the city from the out-lying suburbs.

144

# Transport by Sea and Air

Before roads and railways were built, and for many years afterwards, goods were carried from one port to another by coastal ships. At first there were schooners and scows (flat-bottomed sailing ships which could enter rivers and narrow harbours), but in the course of time they were replaced by small steamers. Some of the later coastal ships were large vessels, well-known to most New Zealanders. In spite of the increasing competition from other forms of transport, a large volume of heavy goods is still carried by coastal cargo vessels; and of course in a country like New Zealand with two large islands, inter-island shipping will always be important. The three rail-ferry steamers that travel between Wellington and Picton every day have

Shipping at the Port of Hokitika in the "Golden Sixties"

*Above:* One of the three ferry steamers of the New Zealand Railways that carries passengers, cars, and railway trucks across Cook Strait between Wellington in the North Island and Picton in the South Island.
*Below:* Passengers driving their cars ashore across the link-span.

146

been designed to carry loaded railway trucks, motor cars, and passengers. The names of the first two are *Aramoana* and *Aranui*—"path across the sea" and "great path". They have indeed made a path between the two islands. Much time and money is saved in freighting goods in this way, because the railways vans no longer have to be unloaded and loaded again at the other terminal.

Water-borne traffic is gradually giving place to road, rail, and air transport. The first official airmail flight was made from Auckland to Dargaville as early as 1919. It was several years before aircraft travel was safe and reliable enough to be used for conveying passengers. Before the second world war, passenger services were running regularly. Today most parts of the country are linked by daily flights, and urgent and perishable goods are carried quickly and economically by plane.

An aeroplane built by the Walsh Brothers at Auckland in the year 1915.

Bristol freighters carry many tonnes of goods from the North Island to the South Island every year. The loads are carried on cargons, which are trays piled high with merchandise that can be wheeled quickly in and out of the open nose doors. This means that one of these cargo planes can be loaded and unloaded in six minutes. In a single day four of these Freighters carried 282 tonnes of cargo in seventy-two flights, which was a world record.

International airports that can handle the big overseas jet aircraft have been made at Auckland and Christchurch, but even the internal services need ever-increasing expenditure on airport control, radio beacons, and radar equipment.

Transport is the very life of the country, and roads, railways, ships, and aircraft have all had a vital part in the development of New Zealand. There will never be a time when they are not needed.

The mighty jet engines of an ANZ plane link New Zealand with the rest of the world. The country is covered by a network of air routes operated by NAC, while flights to Australia and other countries are made daily from the larger airports, bringing New Zealand closer to the rest of the world.

# After World War II

The past quarter of a century, since the end of the Second World War, has made a great difference to New Zealand. The two main islands are joined by strong cables that carry electricity generated in the South Island to the more densely populated North Island. Enormous dams have been constructed on some of the South Island

The natural grandeur of Milford Sound.

rivers to supply water to powerful generating stations, and a mammoth task was undertaken at Lake Manapouri to provide electricity for an aluminium smelting plant. In the North Island underground steam has been harnessed at Wairakei to drive turbines that produce more electricity for the power-hungry industries of our land.

In Taranaki deep wells have been bored into the earth in search of oil and natural gas. At Kapuni natural gas has been discovered and is piped hundreds of kilometres across country to Auckland Wellington, and other places. At Marsden Point, Whangarei, an oil refinery has been built. Oil is imported in a crude state, and refined into petrol and other products, saving a great deal of money that would otherwise have had to be sent overseas—and it is hoped that natural oil will also be found in large quantities.

Managing a country is rather like keeping a proper family budget. The Minister of Finance and various Government Departments must be careful not to spend more than they earn. The early settlers were content to live in a single room, carrying the water they needed from nearby streams, and cooking over an open fire. Nowadays most people live in comfortable homes or flats. They expect to have running water, electricity, radios, TV sets, washing machines and refrigerators in their homes and good wallpapers, and carpets on the floors. Practically all these modern luxuries are made in New Zealand, but huge sums of money have to be spent on the machinery and raw materials from which these things are made, and on manufactured goods that cannot be made locally. Hydro-electric stations and other big national works also cost a great deal for equipment.

Where does all the money come from? Now that ships are able to carry refrigerated cargo to every part of the world, and wool and other farm products can be sent swiftly from one country to another, we might expect that New Zealand could earn as much money as she needs to pay for all the supplies she imports. In the 1960s there were some prosperous years, when wool sold at such a high price that the Government put some of the money away, in case there would come a time when prices fell. In 1967 this drop in prices occurred. The income of the country fell sharply and hundreds of thousands of bales of wool had to be bought by a New Zealand organisation called the Wool Commission, instead of being sold to other countries. These bales were sold slowly during the following years as prices began to rise again.

At the beginning of the 1960s another problem had arisen. Britain

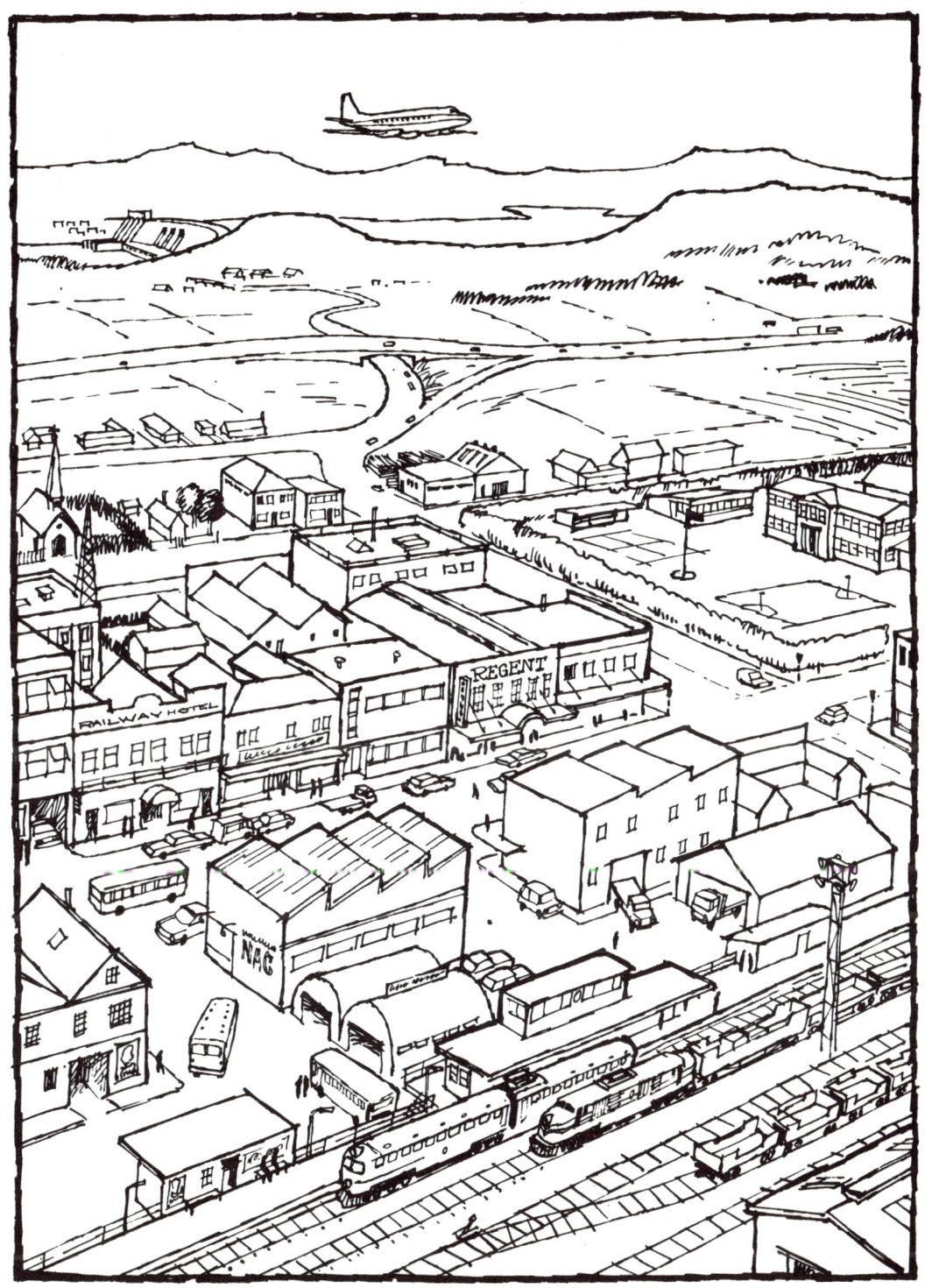

A New Zealand country town of the 1970s. Compare it with the picture on page 136 and see what changes have taken place in the space of fifty or sixty years.

had paid very heavily for the task she had carried through so well in the war. It seemed important to many of her people that it would help her if she join other European countries to form one big trading group. If she did this, it meant that she would have to buy more from Europe and less from New Zealand. Because this would have such a bad effect on New Zealand she promised to try to give special privileges to the little country she had colonised more than a hundred years ago.

Great Britain found that it was not as easy to join the European Economic Community, as the group of countries was called, as she had hoped, but New Zealand had had a fright. Perhaps it was all for the best. For so long she had counted on Britain taking all her primary produce that she had not learned the hard lesson that before you can sell anything you have to go out and sell it. Suddenly the people of New Zealand realised that they must try and sell their primary produce in every part of the world and not just to Britain. To protect themselves even further, they decided to make more manufactured goods and sell them to other countries.

The Government set up offices in many of the important cities of the world to gather information to help New Zealand businessmen when they travel overseas to try to sell their products. Backing them up are the farmers and manufacturers, who are trying to keep quality up and prices down so that New Zealand products will be bought by other countries. While this goes on, the Government still has to take care of what is called the "balance of payments", to ensure that we do not buy more than we sell. It does this in several ways, sometimes by telling business firms how much they can buy, sometimes by telling them how much money they are allowed to send out of the country, and sometimes by borrowing money from overseas.

Different Governments have different ways of controlling the balance of payments. Each of them, National or Labour, has a chance to do it in the way it thinks best if it is elected by the people.

## New Zealand and the World

In 1953 something happened that could hardly have been possible a hundred years before. For the first time in history New Zealand was visited by a reigning monarch, when Queen Elizabeth the Second and her husband, the Duke of Edinburgh arrived in December. In the following month Parliament was opened by Her Majesty, who is the Queen of New Zealand as well as of Britain and other countries in the Commonwealth. It was a reminder that though the British Empire is a thing of the past, the British Commonwealth is made up of people who still look on Great Britain as the Motherland.

They are like sons and daughters who have all left home, but still belong to the same family. They have to look after themselves now, because they can no longer depend on the Motherland to look after them. In business they trade with many different countries. They have also reached a time when they must take care of themselves. In 1954 New Zealand joined Britain, the United States, France, Australia, Pakistan, the Philippines, and Thailand in signing a treaty in which these eight nations have agreed to defend the countries of South-East Asia against attack.

New Zealand has realised that the people of South-East Asia are her neighbours, and that neighbours must help each other. Fighter-bomber and transport squadrons of the Royal New Zealand Air Force and New Zealand Army Units have served in Malaysia, Thailand, Singapore, Korea, and Vietnam. The Government has sent more than a million dollars to these and other countries to help educate their people and to relieve hunger, while many people, and organisations such as CORSO, send gifts of money, food, and clothing. The voice of New Zealand has been heard in the General Assembly of United Nations and the Security Council.

The grandeur of a modern city. Skyscrapers of Wellington with the old wooden Government Building at bottom left.

# New Zealand in the 1970's

New Zealand is still growing. In the city of Auckland the Waitemata Harbour is spanned by a traffic bridge that has opened up the north shore for occupation by the inhabitants of a city of more than half a million people. Newsprint and paper pulp are manufactured for home use or exported to Australia. Millions of metres of timber are milled and sold to Japan each year. Manufacturing industries are growing rapidly and the export of manufactured goods to many foreign countries is also increasing.

There are broadcasts to schools and free textbooks for all primary and secondary school pupils. Universities have been established in several of the principal cities. Television programmes can be received in the majority of New Zealand homes. Oil and mineral exploration is being conducted in several parts of the country, and it is hoped that important discoveries of this kind will help the national economy.

It would be possible to fill many pages with descriptions of New Zealand's natural resources, its temperate climate and scenic beauty, and the accomplishments of its citizens in art, education, commerce, industry, science, and other fields. It is good for us to think of what has been achieved by the inhabitants of a small country in a part of the world far distant from the great continents, but it is equally important to realise the problems and challenges that must be faced in the future.

We have seen how the first inhabitants, both Maori and Pakeha, tamed a new land. The Europeans made mistakes, some of which still have to be paid for, but at least they tackled their problems vigorously.

Maoris and Pakehas work happily together, but there are many well-informed Maoris who believe that the terms of the Treaty of Waitangi have never been properly carried out by Pakehas, and that they have been deprived of some of their rights. Thoughtful people also realise that greater efforts must be made to educate Maori children, to accept older ones on an equal footing in social life, and to learn to appreciate their culture.

In the past New Zealanders have been quick to claim world leadership in social welfare. They were the first to allow women to vote, and to provide old age pensions and other social security benefits, but care of elderly people, and the provision of medical and other benefits has fallen below the standard of several other countries and need to be improved.

At one time several groups of islands in the Pacific were dependencies of New Zealand. Now they have achieved independence, but the New Zealand government must continue to give them assistance that will enable them to govern themselves wisely.

Economic security is a subject of great importance. Britain's membership of the European Economic Community (EEC) has an important effect on this distant part of the Commonwealth. New Zealand must make some changes in its farming and seek new markets. For too long it has depended on Britain as its principal customer. Now it must find new channels both for its farm products and its manufactured goods. The future of the country is almost certain to be more closely connected with the neighbouring lands of Australia and South-east Asia. In the great South-east Asian subcontinent there are a number of developing countries. To these New Zealand has an obligation—to help in defence, agriculture, industry, and education, not only by gifts of money but also by providing technical assistance. These are things she must do to ensure the friendship and support of nations that are growing in strength and importance, and on whom she may need to depend in future years.

A great deal of thought and hard work is already being devoted to these and many other present-day problems. If New Zealand, this small, isolated country at the far ends of the earth, so richly provided with natural resources, is to continue to grow as a nation, she must not remain satisfied with what has been done in the past. Her future depends on how the young people of the present day face up to the problems of the future.

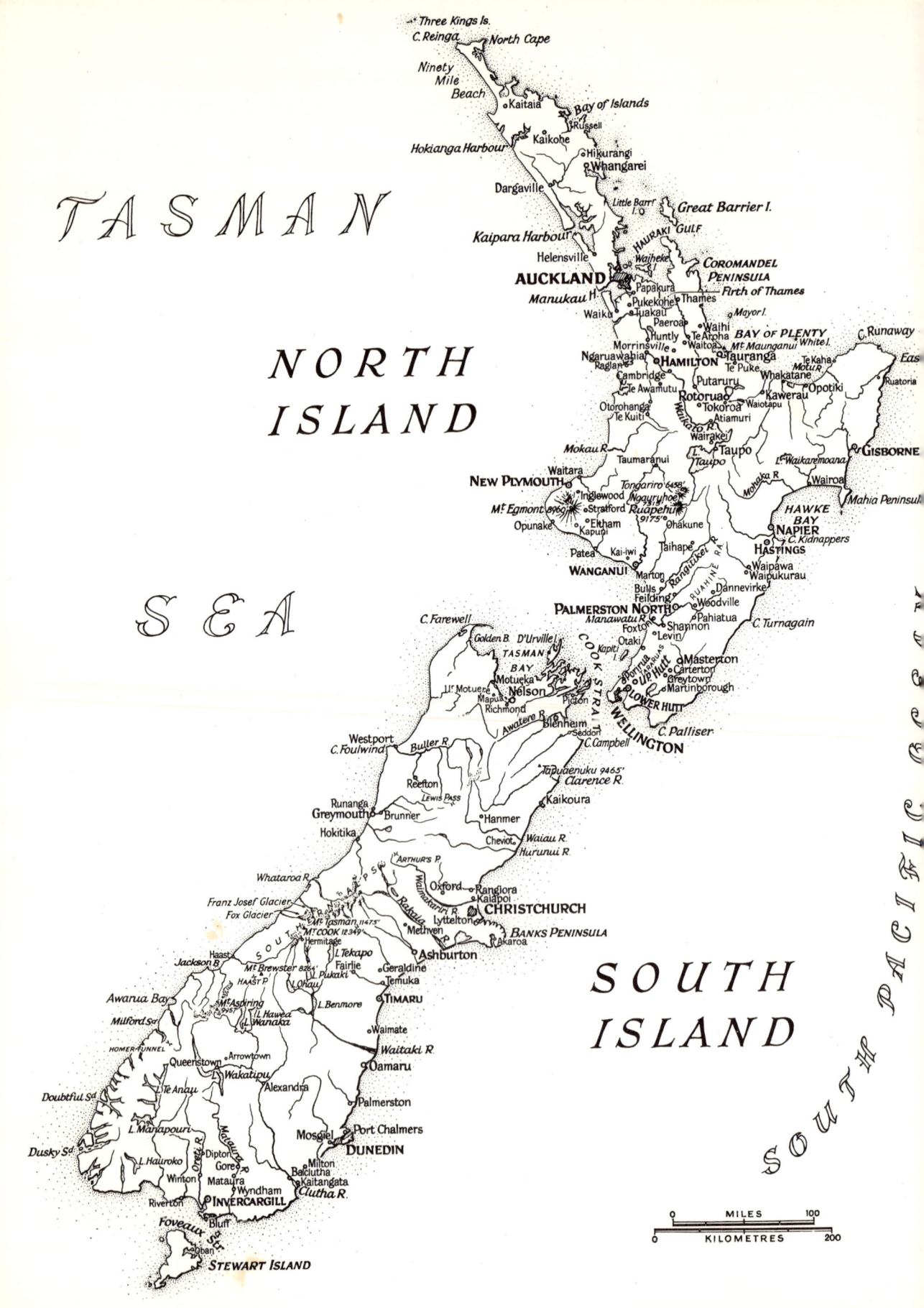

# Index of People, Places, and Ships

## OTHER REED BOOKS

### Pageant of the Pacific Series

Twenty-four page books, with covers in full colour, written for children of 9 to 12 years. Pageants depict life in New Zealand, Australia and the Pacific. Topics range from the coming of the Maoris, to coconut production in the Pacific. They are illustrated throughout with maps, photographs and line drawings.

### Pan Pacific Books

The Pan series investigates at greater depth topics in New Zealand and the Pacific. They too have striking colour covers and profuse illustrations. The Pakeha and Maori Wars, Nuku'alofa, Gold Discoveries in New Zealand—these and many more topics are discussed in simple language at a high level of interest.

### Let's Look at New Zealand

A magnificent pictorial book by A.W. Reed that tells young people (and older ones too) all about New Zealand from her mountains, rivers, lakes, plants and birds to local government, defence, science and how money is earned and spent. It is illustrated in full colour throughout.

### The Story of New Zealand

Written primarily for boys and girls, this popular history by A.H. Reed has become a standard work for all ages. It tells the story of New Zealand from prehistoric times to the present day. There are many photographs, and drawings.

### Seeing New Zealand

D.W. Bircham has written a fully illustrated travel guide that will be an ideal companion for tourists, holiday makers and overseas readers. Magnificent full-colour photographs make this an outstanding attractive description of New Zealand today.

Write to the publishers for full details of all these titles.